RELIGION IN THE PUBLIC SCHOOLS

Published by the
American Association
of School Administrators
1801 N. Moore Street,
Arlington, Virginia
22209-9988

Additional copies of this publication may be ordered from AASA Publications, 1801 N. Moore Street, Arlington, Virginia 22209-9988; 703-528-0700. Price lists and catalogs are available on request.

Religion in the Public Schools, Copyright 1986, American Association of School Administrators, Arlington, Virginia.

Design by Domus Design Studios, Inc.

Library of Congress Number: 86-71778
ISBN: 0-87652-109-X
AASA Stock Number: 21-00174

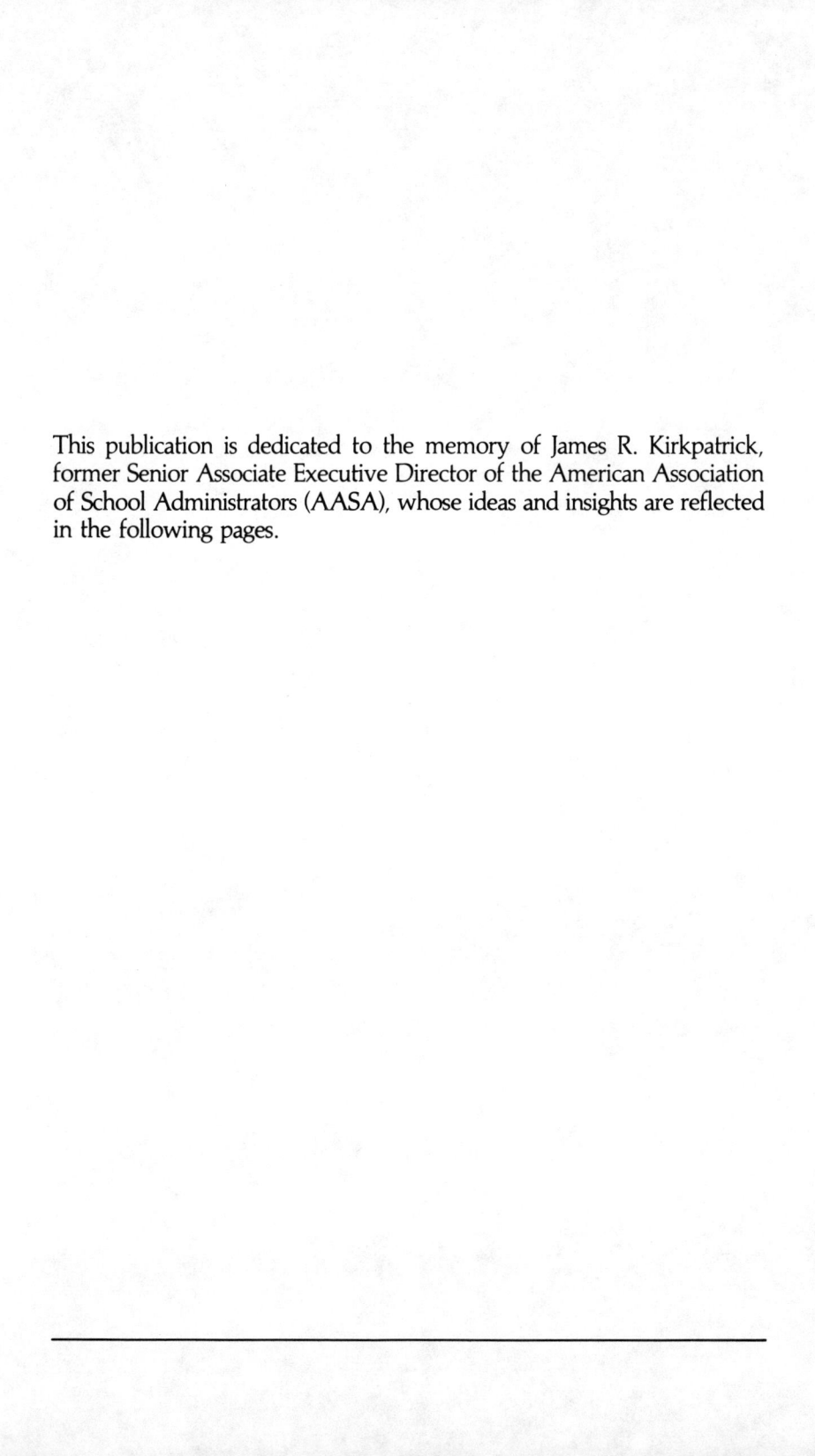

This publication is dedicated to the memory of James R. Kirkpatrick, former Senior Associate Executive Director of the American Association of School Administrators (AASA), whose ideas and insights are reflected in the following pages.

CONTENTS

FOREWORD vii

CHAPTER I   THE ISSUE OF RELIGION IN THE SCHOOLS .. 1

CHAPTER II   THE LAW: ITS BASIS AND IMPLICATIONS

The First Amendment—Religious Freedom; Free Exercise Clause; Establishment Clause; Applications of the Establishment Clause to Religious Activities within the Schools (school-sponsored prayer and devotional bible reading); Aid to Religious Schools; The Religion Clauses and Freedom of Speech 4

CHAPTER III   RELIGION IN THE CURRICULUM

Religious Instruction by Religious Leaders; Teaching About Religions; The Place of Religiously Sensitive Material in the Curriculum (Creationism, "secular humanism," censorship); Excusal 25

CHAPTER IV   RELIGION AND NONCURRICULAR POLICIES OF PUBLIC SCHOOLS

Recognition of Religious Holidays; Other Religious Practices; Extracurricular Bible Study Groups or Clubs; School District Aid to Religious Schools; School-Church Partnerships 47

ACKNOWLEDGMENTS 61

FOREWORD

Effective public schools are essential to the success of our free and democratic society. Religious organizations and groups also make a significant contribution to our society.

Historically, the relationship between the public schools and religious organizations has stimulated discussion, controversy, and cooperation. For decades, the courts have handed down decisions in case after case further defining this sensitive relationship. The struggle to clarify the constitutional separation of church and state is likely to continue.

This book, *Religion in the Public Schools*, is a result of many years of study and research. It is a sourcebook of both law and practice, and should be within reach of every school leader who must, from time to time, deal with this important issue. While additional laws and interpretations of laws are sure to come, this benchmark book will provide essential information for those who need to be conversant with the law and to apply it in their schools.

Partnerships between schools and religious organizations are covered in this publication, which also includes tips for handling a host of perennial concerns, such as baccalaureate ceremonies, observance of religious holidays, excusals, and helping students understand the important role of religion in the shaping of history and human values.

This publication is an indication of AASA's continuing commitment to helping educational leaders and communities deal effectively with important issues. A better understanding of these issues and how to handle them ultimately leads to an even better education for students.

Richard D. Miller, Ph.D.
Executive Director
American Association of School Administrators

CHAPTER I

THE ISSUE OF RELIGION IN THE SCHOOLS

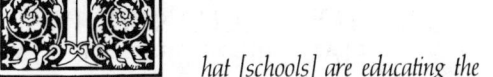

That [schools] are educating the young for citizenship is reason for scrupulous protection of Constitutional freedoms of the individual, if we are not to strangle the free mind at its source and teach youth to discount important principles of our government as mere platitudes.[1]

Public schools are indispensable to American democracy. Their chief responsibility is to develop literate and good citizens for the general and individual welfare. As the Supreme Court has noted, the schools—more than any other institution in society—have a responsibility to demonstrate democracy, not just teach it.

Public schools bring together individuals irrespective of race, creed, color, or wealth. They include more Catholic children than all the Catholic schools combined; they include more Jewish children than all the Jewish schools combined; they include more Protestant children than all the Protestant schools combined; and they include more children of other religious beliefs and denominations than all the schools operated by people of those denominations combined. The public schools include children of all races and children from every national and ethnic background on earth. Indeed, the public schools are at the center of America's multi-faceted culture.

Twenty years ago, AASA's Commission on Religion in the Public Schools was charged with developing a set of guidelines for school administrators who were concerned about how to carry out their Constitutional responsibilities in view of Supreme Court rulings on prayer and

---

1. *West Virginia State Board of Education v. Barnett*, 319 U.S. 624, 637 (1943).

Bible reading in schools. The Commission's recommendations were published in 1964 as *Religion in the Public Schools*. In particular, the book offered guidance to school administrators who wanted to accommodate the religious beliefs of Jewish, atheist, and agnostic—as well as Christian—students.

Since that time, the Supreme Court has been asked to hear a wide range of cases dealing with religion in the public schools. These cases cover many aspects of school administration—curriculum, holiday observances, school budgets, and religious activities held on school premises. Many of these cases have arisen from concerns by some parents that their children's right to free exercise of their religion is being denied.

> "IN THE FACE OF SUCH PROFOUND CHANGES, PRACTICES WHICH MAY HAVE BEEN OBJECTIONABLE TO NO ONE IN THE TIME OF JEFFERSON AND MADISON MAY TODAY BE HIGHLY OFFENSIVE TO MANY PERSONS, THE DEEPLY DEVOUT AND NONBELIEVERS ALIKE."
>
> —Justice Brennan, concurring opinion,
> *Abington School District v. Schempp,*
> 374 U.S. 203, 241 (1963).

Today, more than 20 years after the Supreme Court ruled that school prayers violated the First Amendment, the subject continues to provoke serious debate. A 1983 survey of school administrators and superintendents in North Carolina indicated that prayer was conducted at various times in 31 percent of the public schools and that daily prayer was held in at least one of every six schools.[2]

Schools are also being challenged because they
- teach evolution
- do not allow devotional Bible reading in schools
- are accused of instilling a hidden and pernicious set of values or moral principles called "secular humanism."

---

2. As cited in F.W. English, "Emerging Issues for School Administrators," in *NCRPE Bulletin*, Vol. 10, No. 4, Fall 1983, pp. 64-71; data obtained "N.C. Schools Promote Religion, Study Contends," *Education Week*, September 21, 1983, pp. 3-4. Beginning with Volume 11, the *NCRPE Bulletin* became *Religion & Public Education*.

At the same time when some parents are asking schools to include religious, and specifically Christian, practices in the schools, the public schools—and society itself—have grown increasingly diverse. Today, there are more than 289 denominations listed in the *Handbook of Denominations in the United States.* These range from Adventists to Vadantists; there are Baha'is, Buddhists and 28 denominations of Baptists.[3] There are more Mormons in the United States than there are Presbyterians; there are nearly as many Muslims (2 million) as there are Episcopalians.[4] For school administrators today, the challenge is not only how to accommodate the religious beliefs of children from the Judeo-Christian heritage with those professing no belief. Today, school administrators must also develop policies that accommodate the rich diversity of religious beliefs found in the country.

As Justice Brennan has noted, "The American experiment in public education available to all children has been guided in large measure by the dramatic evolution of the religious diversity among the population which our public schools serve."[5]

This book is designed to offer school administrators guidance on the constitutional foundations of religious freedom and church/state relationships as well as discussion of the most recent Supreme Court cases governing religion in the schools. It considers many of the current issues in the field. It also suggests questions or issues that school administrators may wish to raise before considering any specific policy on this subject.

The public schools have always embodied and fostered the great American dream of liberty and justice for all. The premise of this book is that they can, and will, continue to do so.

---

3. *Handbook of Denominations in the United States,* (New York: Abingdon), 1975.
4. *1985 Yearbook of American and Canadian Churches,* (New York: National Council of Churches of Christ), 1985. Additional estimates provided by the Episcopal Diocese of Virginia and the Islamic Center, Washington, D.C.
5. *Abington School District v. Schempp,* 374 U.S. 203, 241 (1963).

CHAPTER II

THE LAW: ITS BASIS AND IMPLICATIONS

When dealing with questions of religion and other individual liberties guaranteed by the Constitution, schools have a special responsibility to practice what they teach. Public school leaders share with all other governmental officials the obligation to understand and obey the law at every level. In addition, they are entrusted uniquely with the task of transmitting their commitment to the American constitutional form of government by example and education to the children and youth of America.

That responsibility carries with it three obligations for school administrators, first outlined by AASA's Commission on Religion in the Public Schools in 1964:
- To support and defend the Constitution;
- To understand and teach what loyalty to the United States and support for its constitutional form of government involves in citizen rights and duties;
- To distinguish clearly between the citizen's obligation to obey existing law on the one hand, and the inherent right to seek to repeal or amend law through due process on the other.

Today's school administrators still have the responsibility to fulfill those obligations when developing local policies regarding religion in the public schools. Public schools are an arm of the government. The Supreme Court expressed the responsibility of the schools in *Shelton v. Tucker:* "The vigilant protection of constitutional freedoms is nowhere more vital than in the community of American schools."[6]

---

6. 364 U.S. 479, 487 (1960).

It is especially important, then, that school administrators develop local policies in the context of the constitutional freedoms guaranteed to all Americans. An understanding of the First Amendment, which includes constitutional guarantees both of freedom of speech and of religious liberty, is particularly useful.

The Supreme Court has been given the responsibility of interpreting the Constitution and then determining how it applies to specific situations. In many instances, cases arise from situations that may not have been foreseen by those who wrote the Constitution. As a later section of this chapter points out, that is especially true of the relationship between religion and the public schools. Thus the "meaning" of the First Amendment evolves steadily through new Supreme Court decisions applying the law to new situations.

RELIGIOUS FREEDOM

Much of this nation was settled by men and women who came in search of religious freedom. Some colonists—including Puritans, Pennsylvania Dutch, and Quakers—had been persecuted by state-established churches in Europe. Not surprisingly, after the Colonies became independent, the descendants of these first settlers felt that one of the major responsibilities of any new government would be to ensure the preservation of this religious freedom that these diverse sects had found in America. Eight of the original colonies had established churches, and there were established religions in at least four of the other five.[7] Of the eleven colonies that had ratified the Constitution by early 1789, five proposed amendments guaranteeing religious liberty.[8]

James Madison, who was instrumental in writing the Bill of Rights, believed that the most effective way to guarantee religious freedom in the new nation was to preserve religious diversity.

"If there were a majority of one sect," Madison observed, "a Bill of Rights would be a poor protection for liberty. Happily for the United States, they enjoy the utmost freedom of religion. This freedom arises from the multiplicity of sects which pervade America, and which is the best and only security for religious liberty in any society. For where there is such a variety of sects, there cannot be a majority of one sect to oppress and persecute the rest."[9]

---

7. *Engel v. Vitale*, 370 U.S. 421, 427-428 (1962).
8. Justice Rehnquist, dissenting opinion, *Wallace v. Jaffree*, 105 S.Ct. 2479, 2509 (1985).
9. James Madison, quoted in John Swomley, "Church-State Issues in Education," Wingspread Conference on Church/School Partnerships, July 1985, unpublished.

Other members of Congress felt that religious diversity by itself was not enough, and strongly urged that the new Constitution include written guarantees of religious and other individual liberties. In fact, Rhode Island and North Carolina refused to ratify the Constitution unless it included amendments along the lines of those that ultimately became the Bill of Rights.[10]

Madison, who had played a leading role in creating Virginia's Statute of Religious Liberty, first proposed language that eventually became the Religion Clauses of the First Amendment. Madison originally suggested that the amendment read:

> The civil rights of none shall be abridged on account of religious belief or worship, nor shall any national religion be established, nor shall the full and equal rights of conscience be in any manner, or on any pretext, infringed.[11]

The language that Congress finally adopted in December 1791, was written by a conference committee. The guarantees of religious freedom were expressed in these words: "Congress shall make no law respecting an establishment of religion, or prohibiting the free exercise thereof."

Constitutional scholars generally treat the two clauses separately, and often refer to them as the "Establishment Clause" and the "Free Exercise Clause." The Establishment Clause guarantees freedom *from* a state-established religion. The Free Exercise Clause guarantees freedom *of* religion. Much of the time, of course, the two clauses work together to help create the kind of religious liberty Madison envisioned when he drafted the First Amendment. If the majority is not free to establish its religion, then minorities are free to exercise their own religious beliefs.[12]

The Supreme Court itself has noted, however, that there can sometimes be inherent tension between the Establishment Clause and the Free Exercise Clause: "[I]f expanded to a logical extreme, [each] would tend to clash with the other."[13] The Supreme Court added that the task of both "preserv[ing] the autonomy and freedom of religious bodies while avoiding any semblance of established religion" sometimes requires policy makers to walk a "tight rope."[14] Excellent examples of this tension arise, particularly in financial areas such as church tax exemptions.

Since the First Amendment was adopted, constitutional scholars have engaged in extensive debate on exactly what the writers of the

---

10. Justice Rehnquist, *Wallace v. Jaffree*, 105 S.Ct. 2479 (1985), dissenting opinion at 2509.
11. 1 Annals of Congress 434.
12. Thayer S. Warshaw, *Religion, Education and the Supreme Court* (Nashville: Abington, 1979), p. 6.
13. *Walz v. Tax Commission*, 397 U.S. 664, 668-669, (1970).
14. *Ibid.*, at 672.

Constitution did and did not mean by those two clauses. But whatever the members of the first Congress may have been thinking when they wrote the First Amendment, they probably were not considering how it would ultimately affect the relationship between religion and the public schools. "The simple truth," Supreme Court Justice O'Connor once observed,

> is that free public education was virtually non-existent in the late eighteenth century. . . . Since there then existed few government-run schools, it is unlikely that the persons who drafted the First Amendment, or the state legislators who ratified it, anticipated the problems of interaction of church and state in the public schools.[15]

Nevertheless, today's school administrators do have to deal with those problems. In the last century—and increasingly during the last few decades—parents, students, and school administrators have raised numerous questions about how to apply the First Amendment to the schools. No institution in society has been asked to walk the constitutional "tight rope" between the two Religion Clauses more frequently than the public schools.

The Court[16] itself has noted that, "it is far easier to agree on the purpose that underlies the First Amendment's Establishment and Free Exercise Clauses than to obtain agreement on the standards that should govern their application."[17] Nonetheless, some general standards have been developed. This chapter outlines some of the most important Supreme Court cases that have established a framework within which schools and school districts must operate.

I CONTEMPLATE WITH SOVEREIGN REVERENCE THAT ACT OF THE WHOLE AMERICAN PEOPLE WHICH DECLARED THAT THEIR LEGISLATURE SHOULD "MAKE NO LAW RESPECTING AN ESTABLISHMENT OF RELIGION, OR PROHIBITING THE FREE EXERCISE THEREOF," THUS BUILDING A WALL OF SEPARATION BETWEEN CHURCH AND STATE.

—President Thomas Jefferson (1802)
Letter to the Danbury Baptist Association

---

15. *Wallace v. Jaffree*, 105 S.Ct. 2479, concurring opinion at 2503 (1985).
16. This book follows the generally accepted practice of using "Court" to refer to the Supreme Court and "court" to refer to all lower courts.
17. *Walz v. Tax Commission*, 397 U.S. 664, 694 (1970).

THE FIRST AMENDMENT APPLIES TO STATE AND LOCAL GOVERNMENT

The wording of the Religion Clauses of the First Amendment indicates they refer only to the federal government: "Congress shall make no law respecting an establishment of religion, or prohibiting the free exercise thereof."

State governments and local units of government such as school districts are nonetheless subject to the provisions of the First Amendment.

When the Fourteenth Amendment was added to the Constitution, it prohibited any state from depriving any person of liberty without due process of law. One such protected liberty was the freedom of religion protected by the First Amendment. Thus the Court ruled that the Fourteenth Amendment applies the First Amendment to the states and through them to local governments as well.

FREE EXERCISE CLAUSE

The first clause of the First Amendment has most typically been cited by members of religious minorities seeking to preserve what they considered to be their right to free exercise of their religion. It is useful to view this freedom on three levels—the right to *believe*, the right to *advocate* one's beliefs, and the right to *practice* one's religion.

The right to *believe* has always been held to be absolute. James Madison, one of the strongest proponents of this philosophy, noted in 1784 that "in matters of religion no man's right is abridged by the institution of civil society."[18]

Because our nation affords such primacy to the right to believe, there have been relatively few cases dealing with this issue. As the Supreme Court noted in *Braunfeld v. Brown*, "compulsion by law of the acceptance of any creed or the practice of any form of worship is strictly forbidden. The freedom to hold religious beliefs and opinions is absolute."[19]

The Court has been asked to rule on a few cases dealing with the right to believe. For example, the state of Maryland would not allow a man to become a notary public unless he declared his belief in the existence of God. The Court held that the requirement violated freedom

---

18. James Madison, "A Memorial and Remonstrance Against Religious Assessments," 1784, appendix to *Everson v. Board of Education*, 330 U.S. 1, 63-72 (1946).
19. *Braunfeld v. Brown*, 366 U.S. 599, 603 (1961).

of belief: "neither a State nor the Federal Government can constitutionally force a person to profess a belief or disbelief in any religion."[20]

Another important case grew out of a West Virginia law that required all students to give the Pledge of Allegiance. Some students, who were Jehovah's Witnesses, found that this requirement forced them to profess something that they did not believe because it conflicted with their religion. The Court struck down the requirement, noting that the Bill of Rights had not "left it open to public authorities to compel [an individual] to utter what is not in his mind."[21]

> "IF THERE IS ANY FIXED STAR IN OUR CONSTITUTIONAL CONSTELLATION, IT IS THAT NO OFFICIAL, HIGH OR PETTY, CAN PRESCRIBE WHAT SHALL BE ORTHODOX IN POLITICS, NATIONALISM, RELIGION OR OTHER MATTERS OF OPINION OR FORCE CITIZENS TO CONFESS BY WORD OR ACT THEIR FAITH THEREIN."
> —Justice Jackson, majority opinion,
> *Board of Education v. Barnette,*
> 319 U.S. 624, 642 (1943).

The right to *advocate* one's religious beliefs also ordinarily is given the highest level of protection. Freedom to advocate religious beliefs is closely linked to the right of free speech. But the freedom to advocate one's beliefs can be restricted under certain limited circumstances. There can be reasonable regulation of the time, place, and manner of advocating one's beliefs in public places, if the regulation is reasonably related to a legitimate public goal. For example, the right to advocate one's beliefs does not encompass the right to advocate them on a bullhorn in a residential neighborhood at 6 a.m. The individual's interest in advocating beliefs must be balanced against the public interest in peace and quiet. In general, such regulation must be applied even-handedly, by reference to reasonable standards. A law that gave local officials unfettered discretion to grant or deny permission to religious groups that wanted to do door-to-door canvassing was held unconstitutional. The Court concluded

---
20. *Torcaso v. Watkins,* 367 U.S. 488, 495 (1961).
21. *West Virginia Board of Education v. Barnette,* 319 U.S. 624 (1943).

> "WE BEGIN WITH THE PROPOSITION THAT THE RIGHT OF FREEDOM OF THOUGHT PROTECTED BY THE FIRST AMENDMENT AGAINST STATE ACTION INCLUDES BOTH THE RIGHT TO SPEAK FREELY AND THE RIGHT TO REFRAIN FROM SPEAKING AT ALL.... THE RIGHT TO SPEAK AND THE RIGHT TO REFRAIN FROM SPEAKING ARE COMPLEMENTARY COMPONENTS OF THE BROADER CONCEPT OF 'INDIVIDUAL FREEDOM OF MIND.'"
>
> —Chief Justice Burger, majority opinion,
> *Wooley v. Maynard,*
> 430 U.S. 705, 714 (1977).

that such discretion could too easily be abused to control the content of the advocacy.[22]

The right to *practice* one's religion is also very stringently protected, but it has been limited in some cases. As early as 1879, the Supreme Court held that claims of religious liberty were not absolute if there were a compelling public interest in preventing certain religious practices.[23] The Court, citing Thomas Jefferson's statement that the First Amendment erected a "wall of separation"[24] between church and state, said that:

> Congress was deprived of all legislative power over mere opinion, but was left free to reach *actions* which were in violation of social duties or subversive of good order... Suppose one believed that human sacrifice were a necessary part of religious worship, would it be seriously contended that a civil government under which he lived could not interfere to prevent a sacrifice? [emphasis added][25]

The Court has used this same reasoning to uphold state laws outlawing the handling of poisonous snakes during religious services. In essence, the Court in such cases has said that people are free to *believe* that they should, for example, handle poisonous snakes in religious services, but they are not necessarily free to *do* so.

---

22. *Cantwell v. Connecticut,* 310 U.S. 296 (1940).
23. *Reynolds v. United States,* 98 U.S. 145 (1879).
24. Jefferson also wrote that "the legislative powers of government reach actions only and not opinions." Thomas Jefferson, cited in *Braunfeld v. Brown,* 366 U.S. 599, 604 (1961).
25. *Ibid.,* at 164, 166.

For educators, the most common application of this reasoning has been in upholding state laws that require students to be vaccinated against certain infectious diseases before they attend school, even if such vaccinations are contrary to their religious beliefs. The principle was well expressed in an Ohio case, in which the state supreme court said:

> Under the First Amendment of our Constitution, freedom to believe in and to adhere to one's chosen form of religion cannot be restricted by law, but freedom to act in accordance with one's religious beliefs necessarily "remains subject to regulation for the protection of society."[26]

One scholar has summarized the Court's treatment of the practice of religion under the Free Exercise Clause as follows: a religious practice is constitutionally protected if it can pass these tests:

- It must be dictated directly by religious beliefs that are sincerely held;
- It must not seriously interfere with a compelling or overriding state interest; or
- That state interest may be achieved by an alternative method that does not restrict the religious practice.[27]

One example of the application of these principles arose in a Wisconsin case. Old Order Amish parents were tried and convicted of violating the state's compulsory school attendance law, which required them to see that their children attended public or private school until reaching the age of 16. The children, ages 14 and 15, had completed the eighth grade. In testimony given during the trial, it was shown that the parents believed, in accordance with their religion, that by sending their children to high school, "they would not only expose themselves to the danger of the censure of the church community, but... also endanger their own salvation and that of their children."[28]

While noting that "[p]roviding public schools ranks at the very apex of the function of a State,"[29] the Supreme Court, however, nonetheless held that in this case, the compulsory attendance law could "gravely endanger if not destroy the free exercise of respondents' religious beliefs."[30]

It is important to note, however, that protection from state regulation in this case applied only because the objection to the regulation was based on religious grounds. "A way of life," the Court noted, "however virtuous and admirable, may not be interposed as a barrier to reasonable state

---

26. *United States v. Willard*, 211 F.Supp. 643, 645 (D. Ohio 1962).
27. Warshaw, *Religion, Education, and the Supreme Court*, unpublished revisions, p. 11.
28. *Wisconsin v. Yoder*, 406 U.S. 205, 209 (1972).
29. *Ibid.*, at 213.
30. *Ibid.*, at 219.

regulation of education if it is based on purely secular considerations; to have the protection of the Religion Clauses, the claims must be rooted in religious belief."[31] For example, the Court suggested that if the parents had based their objections on their own subjective rejection of the values accepted by the majority of society (in the same way that Thoreau rejected the values of his time), they would not be eligible for protection under the First Amendment.

It is also important that the Amish parents were not asking that their children be excused from *all* obligations to attend school. Each of the students had completed the eighth grade, and the Court noted that the Amish have a "long-established program of informal vocational education."[32] Thus the Amish were excused from compulsory school attendance because their objection was based on a sincerely held religious belief, and because it did not interfere unduly with a compelling or overriding state interest.

THE FIRST AMENDMENT HAS...
A DOUBLE ASPECT.
ON THE ONE HAND,
IT FORESTALLS COMPULSION BY LAW
OF THE ACCEPTANCE OF ANY CREED OR THE
PRACTICE OF ANY FORM OF WORSHIP.
FREEDOM OF CONSCIENCE AND FREEDOM TO ADHERE
TO SUCH RELIGIOUS ORGANIZATION OR FORM OF
WORSHIP AS THE INDIVIDUAL MAY CHOOSE
CANNOT BE RESTRICTED BY LAW. ON THE OTHER HAND,
IT SAFEGUARDS THE FREE EXERCISE OF THE
CHOSEN FORM OF RELIGION. THUS THE
AMENDMENT EMBRACES TWO CONCEPTS —
FREEDOM TO BELIEVE AND FREEDOM TO ACT.
THE FIRST IS ABSOLUTE, BUT, IN THE NATURE OF THINGS,
THE SECOND CANNOT BE. CONDUCT REMAINS SUBJECT
TO REGULATION FOR THE PROTECTION OF SOCIETY.

—*Cantwell v. Connecticut*,
310 U.S. 296, 303, 304 (1940).

---

31. *Ibid.*, at 215.
32. *Ibid.*, at 222.

THE STATE AND PRIVATE OR RELIGIOUS SCHOOLS

In a 1925 case, *Pierce v. Society of Sisters*,[33] the Court struck down an Oregon law that required every person having custody of a school-age child to send the child to *public* school. The Court found that the law interfered with parents' "liberty... [to] direct the upbringing and education of [their] children." But the Court also recognized the states' authority to prescribe educational standards for private and religious schools.

ESTABLISHMENT CLAUSE

The main purpose of the Establishment Clause is to ensure governmental neutrality in matters of religion. The Court stated this position most succinctly in a 1971 case: "When government activities touch on the religious sphere, they must be secular in purpose, evenhanded in operation, and neutral in primary impact."[34]

The classic interpretation of the Establishment Clause was written by Justice Black in *Everson v. Board of Education:*

> The "establishment of religion" clause of the First Amendment means at least this: Neither a state nor the Federal Government can set up a church. Neither can pass laws which aid one religion over another. Neither can force nor influence a person to go or to remain away from church against his will or force him to profess a belief or disbelief in any religion. No person can be punished for entertaining or professing religious beliefs or disbeliefs, for church attendance or non-attendance. No tax in any amount... can be levied to support any religious activities or institutions, whatever they may be called, or whatever form they may adopt to teach or practice religion. Neither a state nor the Federal Government can, openly or secretly, participate in the affairs of any religious organizations or groups and vice versa. In the words of Jefferson, the clause against establishment of religion by law was intended to erect "a wall of separation between Church and State."[35]

In a number of cases, courts have been asked to determine whether or not specific school policies violate the Establishment Clause. Justice

---

33. 268 U.S. 510, 534 (1925).
34. *Gillette v. U.S.*, 401 U.S. 437, 450 (1971).
35. 330 U.S. 1, 15-16 (1947).

W̲HEN JUDGE WILLIAM OVERTON OF ARKANSAS DECIDED A CONTROVERSIAL ESTABLISHMENT CLAUSE CASE (*MCLEAN v. ARKANSAS BOARD OF EDUCATION,* DISCUSSED IN GREATER LENGTH IN CHAPTER III), HE RECEIVED MANY CRITICAL LETTERS. THE COMMENTS PROMPTED HIM TO WRITE:

The content of many letters suggests a lack of understanding of the Establishment Clause and what this country is about. The argument was advanced time after time that this is a Christian country, founded by Christians, and in colonial times religion was an integral part of public education. . . . What this position ignores, however, is the fact that many early settlers came here to escape the religious tyranny of the established churches in England and on the Continent. It was partly because the colonies could not reach agreement as to which denomination should be the established church that the prohibition of the Establishment Clause was written. The wisdom of James Madison prevailed when the writers of the Constitution recognized that if the State adopts a religion or religious viewpoint, it degrades from equal rank all those citizens who do not subscribe to that official belief. The Establishment Clause permits our society, which is certainly heterogeneous and pluralistic when it comes to matters of religious belief, to exist in relative harmony. A glance at current news publications demonstrates the effect warring religious sects have in places such as Lebanon, Northern Ireland, Iran and Iraq.

—Reflections on *McLean,* Judge William Overton
NCRPE *Bulletin,* Vol. 10, No. 3, Summer 1983.

Powell noted that:
> Most of the cases coming to this Court raising Establishment Clause questions have involved the relationship between religion and education. Among these religion-education precedents, two general categories may be identified: those dealing with religious activities within the schools, and those involving public aid in varying forms to sectarian educational institutions.[36]

Cases concerning each of these categories will be discussed in turn.

---

36. *Committee for Public Education and Religious Liberty v. Nyquist,* 413 U.S. 756, 772 (1973).

APPLICATIONS OF THE ESTABLISHMENT CLAUSE TO RELIGIOUS ACTIVITIES WITHIN THE SCHOOLS

SCHOOL-SPONSORED PRAYER: ENGEL v. VITALE

School-sponsored prayer and devotional Bible reading in schools are the religious activities that have been the greatest sources of litigation and public confusion concerning application of the Establishment Clause. The first major decision on school-sponsored prayer came in 1962, when the Supreme Court, by a vote of 6 to 1, struck down a state-sponsored program of interdenominational prayer in the public schools of New York.

In that case, the New Hyde Park Board of Education had required all teachers to open each school day with the following prayer: "Almighty God, we acknowledge our dependence upon Thee, and we beg Thy blessings upon us, our parents, our teachers and our country." The school board's policy permitted children who did not wish to participate in the prayer to be excused from taking part.

The Court's decision was handed down in *Engel v. Vitale*. The Court from the outset left no doubt that the New York practice was wholly inconsistent with the Establishment Clause. By its very nature prayer is religious, and the Constitutional prohibition against establishing a religion must at a minimum mean that in the United States "it is not part of the business of government to compose official prayers for any group of the American people to recite as a part of a religious program carried on by government,"[37] the Court stated.

Speaking for the Court, Justice Black went on to explain that the practice violated the Establishment Clause even though no children were compelled to take part.

> The Establishment Clause, unlike the Free Exercise Clause, does not depend on any showing of direct governmental compulsion.... When the power, prestige, and financial support of government is placed behind a particular religious belief, the indirect coercive pressure upon religious minorities to conform to the prevailing officially approved religion is plain.[38]

In other words, excusing students from participating in an activity will not change its basic nature—excusal does not provide an easy way around Establishment Clause questions. (Chapter III contains a more extensive discussion of excusal.)

---

37. 370 U.S. 421, 425 (1962).
38. *Ibid.*, at 430, 431.

The Court rejected the argument that its holding indicated a hostility to religion or to prayer. "Nothing... could be more wrong," the Court insisted, for "the history of man is inseparable from the history of religion."[39] Neither were the founding fathers hostile to religion or prayer. They drafted the First Amendment to "quiet well-justified fears... arising out of an awareness that governments in the past had shackled men's tongues to make them speak only the religious thoughts that government wanted them to speak and to pray only to the God that government wanted them to pray to," the Court explained.[40]

The Court made it clear, however, that nothing in the decision should be construed as discouraging school children from reciting historical documents such as the Declaration of Independence, containing references to the Deity, or singing "officially espoused anthems" that contain the composer's profession of faith in a Supreme Being. "Such patriotic or ceremonial occasions," the Court insisted, "bear no true resemblance to the unquestioned religious exercise that the state of New York has sponsored...."[41]

SCHOOL-SPONSORED PRAYER: WALLACE v. JAFFREE

Since the *Engel* decision, there have been a number of other efforts to reestablish the practice of public school-sponsored prayers. One expert counted at least 200 proposals introduced into the U.S. Congress to overturn the Supreme Court decision on school prayer from 1962-1985.[42]

In a related development, many state legislatures have adopted "moment of silence" laws. In most instances, the State attorney general or State Supreme Court has ruled that these laws violated the Establishment Clause because, despite the working of the law, the legislators' expressed intent was to bring back school-sponsored prayer. The Court has ruled on only one of these laws, an Alabama statute.

In 1978, the state legislature of Alabama required a one-minute period of silence in all public schools "for meditation." In 1981, the legislature amended the statute to authorize a period of silence "for meditation or voluntary prayer." In 1982, the legislature authorized teachers to lead "willing students" in a prescribed prayer to "Almighty God the Creator and Supreme Judge of the world." Students who objected to the prayer were to be excused from participation.

---

39. *Ibid.*, at 434.
40. *Ibid.*, at 435.
41. *Ibid.*, n. 21, at 435.
42. James E. Wood, "Church-State Issues in Education in the 1980s," *Religion & Public Education*, Vol. 12, No. 3, Summer 1985, p. 77.

A resident of Mobile County, Alabama, filed a complaint on behalf of three of his children after they reported to him that their teachers led prayers in schools. He challenged only the latter two statutes. The state-prescribed prayer was struck down by an appellate court, which found that it was squarely prohibited by *Engel v. Vitale*. Thus the Court was asked to rule on only the narrow question of whether the Alabama law authorizing a period of silence for "meditation or voluntary prayer," enacted to encourage prayer, was a law violating the Establishment Clause of the First Amendment.

In testimony presented to the trial court, the law's chief sponsor, when asked whether his legislation had any goal other than prayer in the schools, replied that he had "no other purpose in mind."[43]

In June of 1985, the Supreme Court, in a 6-3 decision, struck down the law. The Court found that Alabama's 1981 law violated the Establishment Clause because it had as its "sole purpose" encouraging religious activity in the classroom. The Court also found that the legislature had "intended to characterize prayer as a favored practice. Such an endorsement is not consistent with the established principle that the government must pursue a course of complete neutrality toward religion."[44] Writing for the Court, Justice Stevens expanded on what the Court means by religious neutrality:

> Just as the right to speak and the right to refrain from speaking are complementary components of a broader concept of individual freedom of mind, so also the individual's freedom to choose his own creed is the counterpart of his right to refrain from accepting the creed established by the majority. . . .
>
> [T]he Court has unambiguously concluded that the individual freedom of conscience protected by the First Amendment embraces the right to select any religious faith or none at all. This conclusion derives support not only from the interest in respecting the individual's freedom of conscience, but also from the conviction that religious beliefs worthy of respect are the product of free and voluntary choice by the faithful, and from recognition of the fact that the political interest in forestalling intolerance extends beyond intolerance among Christian sects, or even intolerance among "religions," to encompass intolerance of the disbeliever and the uncertain.[45]

---

43. *Wallace v. Jaffree*, 105 S.Ct. 2479, 2483 (1985).
44. *Ibid.*, at 2493.
45. *Ibid.*, at 2488, 2489.

At the same time, one Justice suggested that other "moment of silence" laws, without the clearly religious legislative history of the Alabama law, might be constitutionally permissible.

A state-sponsored moment of silence in the public schools is different from state-sponsored vocal prayer or Bible reading. First, a moment of silence is not inherently religious. Silence, unlike prayer or Bible reading, need not be associated with a religious exercise. Second, a pupil who participates in a moment of silence need not compromise his or her beliefs. . . . It is difficult to discern a serious threat to religious liberty from a room of silent, thoughtful schoolchildren.[46]

It is important to note that in neither the New York nor the Alabama case did the Supreme Court rule "voluntary prayer" unconstitutional. In fact, one of the main reasons the Court objected to both the spoken prayer in *Engel v. Vitale* and the silent prayer in *Wallace v. Jaffree* was they were not voluntary—there was the element of implied coercion that is inherent in any state-sponsored religious exercise. Furthermore, the Court did not rule that religion was not to be discussed in the public schools. "It is neither sacrilegious nor antireligious," the Court said, "to say that each separate government in this country should stay out of the business of writing or sanctioning official prayers."[47]

> "NOTHING IN THE UNITED STATES CONSTITUTION AS INTERPRETED BY THIS COURT. . . PROHIBITS PUBLIC SCHOOL STUDENTS FROM VOLUNTARILY PRAYING AT ANY TIME BEFORE, DURING, OR AFTER THE SCHOOL DAY."
>
> —Justice O'Connor, concurring opinion,
> *Wallace v. Jaffree*,
> 105 S.Ct. 2479 (1985).

DEVOTIONAL BIBLE READING: ABINGTON SCHOOL DISTRICT v. SCHEMPP

The practice of opening the school day with a devotional reading from the Bible was widespread in early America. In fact, the nation's first law requiring communities to establish public schools was "Ye Olde Deluder

---

46. *Ibid.*, at 2498, 2499.
47. *Engel v. Vitale*, at 435.

Satan Act," established by the Massachusetts Bay Colony as a means of ensuring that all young people would be exposed to the Bible's message.

Horace Mann, secretary of the Massachusetts board of education, required public school teachers in Massachusetts to begin each school day with the reading "without comment" of ten verses from the King James Version of the Bible. The practice was followed widely, not only in Massachusetts but throughout the United States.

Mann believed that the Bible reading was a way to help students develop "reason and religious conscience." Non-Protestants, however, who did not accept the King James version of the Bible, sought ways to prevent their children from being exposed to these forms and methods of religious teachings in school. As increasing numbers of Roman Catholic, Eastern Orthodox, and Jewish children arrived in the United States, controversies over Bible readings became more pronounced. In Cincinnati, for example, violence over what version of the Bible would be read in the public schools became known as the Rifle War.[48] During this period, many immigrant groups founded religious schools as a way to preserve their religion, their language, and their culture.

By the late nineteenth and early twentieth century, however, the percentage of children enrolled in the public schools increased dramatically. In 1890, for example, only about 44 percent of all children between the ages of 5 and 17 were enrolled in public schools; but by 1930 that percentage had jumped to 67 percent. And because of immigration, the student body was not only larger but also more heterogeneous. Although the public schools instituted many changes to accommodate the new students, some things did not change. The practice of devotional Bible reading in public schools continued into the 1960s.

In 1963, the Supreme Court agreed to rule on the constitutionality of devotional Bible reading in schools. Two cases from two states—Pennsylvania and Maryland—were involved, but because of the similarity in the state laws, the Supreme Court treated them as one case. The Pennsylvania statute required that:

> At least ten verses of the Holy Bible shall be read, without comment, at the opening of each public school on each school day. Any child shall be excused from such Bible reading, upon the written request of his parent or guardian.[49]

By an 8-to-1 vote, the Supreme Court held that such laws and practices violated the Establishment Clause of the First Amendment as applied to the states by the Fourteenth Amendment. Speaking for the

---

48. Nicholas Piediscalzi, "Studying Religion in the Public Schools," *Church & State*, November 1981, p. 14.
49. *Abington School District v. Schempp*, 374 U.S. 203, 205 (1963).

Court, Justice Clark acknowledged that "religion has been closely identified with our history and government."[50] He went on to explain: "This is not to say, however, that religion has been so identified with our history and government that religious freedom is not likewise as strongly embedded in our public and private life."[51]

Quoting Justice Rutledge's dissenting opinion in an earlier case, the Court explained that:

> The [First] Amendment's purpose was not to strike merely at the official establishment of a single... religion.... It was to create a complete and permanent separation of the spheres of religious activity and civil authority by comprehensively forbidding every form of public aid or support for religion.[52]

Justice Clark emphasized the First Amendment's requirement that the government remain neutral to religion, in the following words:

> This wholesome "neutrality"... stems from a recognition of the teachings of history that powerful sects or groups might bring about a fusion of governmental and religious functions... to the end that official support of... Government would be placed behind the tenets of one or of all orthodoxies.[53]

The Court then fashioned a test to determine whether a state law or practice violated the Establishment Clause. The test was: "What are the purposes and primary effect of the enactment?" The First Amendment is violated, the Court said, "if either [the purpose or primary effect of the law] is the advancement or inhibition of religion."[54]

The Court struck down the laws in question because they had the primary or principle effect of advancing religion. Quite simply, the Court said that laws that were struck down required religious exercises as part of the curricular activities of students who were required by law to attend school.[55]

Then the Court considered and rejected a number of anticipated criticisms of their decision. "It is no defense," the Court noted, "to urge that the religious practices here may be relatively minor encroachments on the First Amendment. The breach of neutrality that is today a trickling stream may all too soon become a raging torrent."[56] Quoting Madison,

---

50. *Ibid.*, at 212.
51. *Ibid.*, at 214.
52. *Everson v. Board of Education*, 330 U.S. 1, 31-32 (1947).
53. 374 U.S. 203, 222 (1963).
54. *Ibid.*
55. *Ibid.*, at 223-24.
56. *Ibid.*, at 225.

the Court emphasized that "it is proper to take alarm at the first experiment on our liberties."[57]

The Court rejected "unequivocally" the contention that the Establishment Clause forbids "only government preference of one religion over another."[58]

The states contended that the Bible was used either as an "instrument for non-religious moral inspiration, or as a reference for the teaching of secular subjects." But as Justice Clark observed, "surely the place of the Bible as an instrument of religion cannot be gainsaid."[59]

Justice Clark denied that the decision would establish a "religion of secularism" in the schools. He went on to say that "one's education is not complete without a study of comparative religion or the history of religion."[60] Moreover, the Court saw the study of the literary and historic qualities of the Bible as worthy.

Finally, the Court rejected the argument that to prohibit a religious exercise approved by the majority would collide with the majority's right to free exercise of religion. The Free Exercise Clause "has never meant that a majority could use the machinery of the state to practice its beliefs."[61]

AID TO RELIGIOUS SCHOOLS

From the time when parochial schools were first established, some state governments provided some forms of public support. Questions over the legality of such aid have provided a number of tests of the Establishment Clause.

In these cases, the Supreme Court has generally held that what is required is official neutrality on subjects of religion—that laws must neither support nor be hostile to religion. The Court established a three-part test, articulated most completely in *Lemon v. Kurtzman*,[62] as a way of determining whether or not a policy or law is neutral on the subject of religion.

In order to be constitutionally permissible, a statute or practice:

- must have a *secular legislative purpose*
- must have a principal or primary *effect of neither advancing nor inhibiting religion*

---

57. James Madison, "Memorial and Remonstrance Against Religious Assessments," quoted in *Everson v. Board of Education*, 330 U.S. 1, 65 (1947).
58. 374 U.S. 203, 216 (1963).
59. *Ibid.*, at 224.
60. *Ibid.*, at 225. A more complete version of Justice Clark's thinking on this subject is included in Chapter III.
61. *Ibid.*, at 226.
62. 403 U.S. 602 (1971).

- must not foster *"excessive government entanglement with religion."* [emphasis added][63].

The relationship between government public and religious schools has led to extensive litigation during the last 40 years. The earliest case was *Everson v. Board of Education*[64], decided by the Supreme Court in 1947. The state legislature of New Jersey had passed a law permitting the use of public funds to pay for the bus transportation of parochial school students to and from parochial schools. One school district in the state implemented the law in a regulation authorizing public funds to be paid to transport students to Roman Catholic parochial schools. The local regulation and state statute were challenged on the ground that they violated the Establishment Clause of the First Amendment.

In its opinion, the Court quoted Jefferson's famous words regarding the purpose of the Establishment Clause, noting that it "was intended to erect 'a wall of separation between church and state.' " Nonetheless, the 5-4 majority of the Court concluded that providing public funds for transportation of parochial school students was not aid to religion—but aid to students. Such a program did not violate the First Amendment since it was designed to promote the safety and welfare of the child, not to aid a religion.

Since that first case, the Supreme Court has faced a number of other cases on the issue of how much aid and what kind of public funds government might provide to students in parochial schools without violating the Establishment Clause.

For example, the Court has held that public schools may lend secular textbooks to students in religious schools.[65] Public schools may also provide diagnostic services in religious schools.[66] Public funds may provide subsidies for recordkeeping that is required by the state.[67] The Court has also upheld a Minnesota law permitting parents to take state income tax deductions for their children's public *and* nonpublic educational expenses, including textbooks and school supplies.[68] All these have been deemed as providing primarily aid to *students*, not aid to *religion*. Some Court observers view these decisions as an *accommodation* of the right to free exercise of religion.

On the other hand, the Supreme Court has struck down a variety of other kinds of aid: providing tax credits for nonpublic school tuition;[69]

---

63. Ibid., at 612-613.
64. 330 U.S. 1 (1947).
65. *Board of Education v. Allen*, 392 U.S. 236 (1968).
66. *Wolman v. Walter*, 433 U.S. 229 (1977).
67. *Committee for Public Education and Religious Liberty v. Regan*, 444 U.S. 648 (1980).
68. *Mueller v. Allen*, 463 U.S. 388 (1983).
69. *Committee for Public Education and Religious Liberty v. Nyquist*, 413 U.S. 756 (1973).

paying for busing on nonpublic school field trips[70]; maintaining and repairing nonpublic schools[71]; and lending equipment or materials that would remain in the school and not be taken home with students.[72] In these cases, the Court has reemphasized the need for *separation* between religion and the state.

Today, many school districts must make decisions about whether to provide aid and what type of aid to provide to nonpublic schools or their students. This issue, particularly the issue of instructional aid, is discussed in greater detail in Chapter IV.

THE RELIGION CLAUSES AND FREEDOM OF SPEECH

The First Amendment provides more than a guarantee of religion liberty. It also provides that Congress may pass no law "abridging the freedom of speech, or of the press" or of assembly. Many times, the distinction between freedom of religion and freedom of speech is difficult to make.

One example of the close relationship between the two is *West Virginia Board of Education v. Barnette*[73], in which students had objected to a compulsory flag salute on the ground that such a practice violated their Jehovah's Witness faith. In its decision, however, the Court dealt with all the freedoms guaranteed in the First Amendment. Justice Jackson, writing for the Court, observed:

> The very purpose of the Bill of Rights was to withdraw certain subjects from the vicissitudes of political controversy, to place them beyond the reach of majorities and officials and to establish them as legal principles applied by the courts. One's right to life, liberty, and property, to free speech, a free press, worship and assembly and other fundamental rights may not be submitted to a vote; they depend on the outcome of no elections.[74]

Subsequently, the Court has upheld the right of other students to be excused from saluting the flag for philosophical, not religious, reasons.

One Supreme Court case, *Tinker v. Des Moines Independent Community School District*[75], clearly establishes students' rights to free speech and similar forms of expression. During the height of the Vietnam war, three students were suspended from school for wearing black armbands

---

70. *Wolman v. Walter*, 433 U.S. 229 (1977).
71. *Committee for Public Education and Religious Liberty v. Nyquist*, 413 U.S. 756 (1973).
72. *Meek v. Pittenger*, 421 U.S. 349 (1975).
73. 319 U.S. 624 (1943).
74. *Ibid.*, at 638.
75. 393 U.S. 503 (1969).

in violation of school policy. The Court overturned the suspensions, ruling that "students or teachers [do not] shed their constitutional rights to freedom of speech or expression at the schoolhouse gate."[76] The Court ruled that unless students' free expression substantially and materially interferes with the requirement of appropriate discipline or invades the rights of others, it cannot be prohibited. The case has been cited more than 500 times on issues of student and nonstudent expression.

The issue of prior restraint of free speech for specifically religious reasons has also been decided. In *Burstyn v. Wilson* [77], the Court held unconstitutional a New York State statute that authorized the state to refuse to permit the showing of any moving picture films that were found to be "obscene, indecent, immoral, inhuman, (or) sacrilegious. . . ." The Court made it clear that a state could not censor films because they might be sacrilegious. If this were permitted, the state would be required to determine what is religion in order to judge what is sacrilegious. The Court noted that "the state has no legitimate interest in protecting any or all religions from views distasteful to them which is sufficient to justify prior restraint upon the expression of these views."[78]

Thus it is important for school administrators to be aware of what the Supreme Court has said on the subject of students' rights to free speech and freedom of expression, particularly when questions of textbook censorship or removal of objectionable material from school library shelves arise. One important case is discussed in Chapter III in the section on "Censorship."

SUMMARY

This discussion has by no means dealt with every issue that the Court has considered. It does, however, set out a basic framework of the Constitution's religion clauses. This framework should provide guidelines for subsequent discussions on religion in the curriculum and other religious practices of schools.

The most important *caveat*, however, is a tendency toward oversimplification and comes from the words of Justice Jackson. The subject of religion in the public schools is one of "magnitude, intricacy and delicacy." The subsequent discussion of religious practices in the schools should be read with that thought in mind.

---

76. *Ibid.*, at 506.
77. 343 U.S. 495 (1952).
78. *Ibid.*, at 505.

CHAPTER III

RELIGION IN THE CURRICULUM

As the previous chapter has shown, the Supreme Court has repeatedly struck down school policies that promote the *practice* of religion during the school day. Nevertheless, it is important to note that the Court has never issued any rulings prohibiting studying about religions in the public schools. In fact, the Court has upheld two very different approaches to teaching about religions in the public schools.

RELIGIOUS INSTRUCTION BY RELIGIOUS LEADERS

In 1952, the Court heard *Zorach v. Clauson*, a case dealing with a New York City practice of dismissing students from school during regular school hours to attend religious education programs *held off school premises in religious institutions*. Students who did not wish to participate in the religious education were required to remain in school. The Court found that this practice *did not* violate the Establishment Clause. The Court stated:

> The First Amendment... does not say that in every and all respects there shall be a separation of Church and State. Rather, it studiously defines the manner, the specific ways, in which there shall be no concert or union or dependency one on the other.... When the state encourages religious instruction or cooperates by adjusting the schedule of public events to sectarian needs, it follows the best of our traditions. For it then respects the religious nature of our people and accommodates the public service to their spiritual needs. To hold that it may not

do so would be to find in the Constitution a requirement that the government show a callous indifference to religious groups. That would be preferring those who believe in no religion over those who do believe.[79]

Justice Douglas explained that separation of church and state does not "mean that public institutions can make no adjustments of their schedules to accommodate the religious needs of the people. We cannot read into the Bill of Rights such a philosophy of hostility to religion."[80]

In contrast, just a few years earlier,[81] the Court had ruled that a released time religious education program *in which classes were held on school property* violated the Establishment Clause. The Court held that in such a program

> the State's tax-supported public school buildings [are] used for the dissemination of religious doctrines. The State also affords sectarian groups an invaluable aid in that it helps to provide pupils for their religious classes through use of the State's compulsory public machinery. This is not separation of Church and State.[82]

In other words, the Court did not find that the Establishment Clause prevented schools from *accommodating* religious education—even religious training—during school hours. What the Court did find impermissible was a program that allowed specific religious beliefs to be advanced on school premises.

In a concurring opinion, Justice Jackson emphasized that there is a place in the school curriculum—and in the school building itself—for objective study of religion:

> Certainly a course in English literature that omitted the Bible and other powerful uses of our mother tongue for religious ends would be pretty barren. And I should suppose it is a proper, if not indispensable, part of preparation for a worldly life to know the roles that religion and religions have played in the tragic story of mankind.[83]

TEACHING ABOUT RELIGIONS

Teaching about religions, as the *McCollum* case illustrates, is constitutionally permissible. In addition, it is sound educational policy. One of the

---

79. 343 U.S. 306, 312-314 (1952).
80. *Ibid.*, at 315.
81. *McCollum v. Board of Education of Champaign, Illinois*, 333 U.S. 203 (1948).
82. *Ibid.*, at 212.
83. *Ibid.*, at 236.

principal roles of the public schools is studying our culture and passing on the rich heritage of the American people. Religions have played a significant part in that cultural heritage.

The Supreme Court has emphasized that there is a place for the study of religions in the public school curriculum. It has also established some basic guidelines for appropriate ways to include the topic of religion in the school curriculum:

[I]t might well be said that one's education is not complete without a study of comparative religion or the history of religion and its relationship to the advancement of civilization. . . . Nothing we have said here indicates that such study of the Bible or of religion, when presented *objectively as part of a secular program of education,* may not be effected consistently with the First Amendment. . . . [emphasis added][84]

In the early 1970s, a number of school districts included some academic study of religions in the curriculum. After a decline in the early 1980s, there is renewed interest in the subject. In general, school districts are looking for programs that distinguish between *teaching* religion and teaching *about* religions.

A leader in the movement to incorporate teaching about religions in the public schools has been the National Council on Religion and Public Education (NCRPE), which provides a "forum and means for cooperation among individuals, organizations, and institutions concerned with those ways of studying religion which are educationally appropriate and constitutionally acceptable to a secular program of public education."[85]

School districts have adopted a wide variety of ways to bring academic study about religions into their secular curriculum. Some have added entire courses. Others have incorporated units on religion and religious influence into existing courses. In some districts, religions are studied as part of the social studies curriculum, while in others, students explore religious influences in the arts and literature. There are at least three major trends in teaching about religions in American schools.

The first is an objective study of religions, generally included as part of the social studies curriculum. In St. Louis Park, Minnesota, for example, secondary school students can elect a half-year social studies course called "Religions in Human Culture." Students in this course study the beliefs and practices of five of the world's major religions: Buddhism, Christianity, Hinduism, Islam, and Judaism. Students also examine the influence these religions have had on various cultures throughout the

---

84. *Abington School District v. Schempp,* 374 U.S. 203, 225 (1963).
85. National Council on Religion and Public Education, statement of purpose. (1300 Oread Street, Lawrence, KS 66045).

world. Curriculum materials developed for this course have been distributed through the National Diffusion Network to schools in all 50 states.

In other school districts, social studies teachers may incorporate one or more units on religions into existing courses. A unit on the Reformation may be included in a world history course. American history courses may include a section on Puritanism. A study of the rise of Islamic fundamentalism may be incorporated into a course on modern world history.

In 1964, AASA's Commission on Religion in the Public Schools noted the "meagerness of the material available that is truly objective, balanced, and educationally sound." Since that time, a number of curriculum development projects have created materials that meet those goals.

The National Council for the Social Studies has issued a strong statement of support for including a study of religions within the social studies curriculum. The statement (see page 33) notes that knowledge about religions "is absolutely necessary for understanding and living in a world of diversity."

A second major trend is an increased involvement of students in exploring religious influences on art and literature, as well as studying such religious works as the Bible for their artistic and literary content. It is virtually impossible to understand the development of civilization without some understanding of the great religious influences reaching back to the earliest of recorded times.

Many teachers of arts and humanities show their students how religious beliefs have influenced the development of various art forms. Theater classes often begin with a study of Greek drama—the foundation of Western theatre—which was developed for religious festivals. Art students learn that African art often has a religious, as well as an aesthetic, purpose. Music classes frequently include the study and performance of religious music, from compositions by Bach to Afro-American spirituals.

English teachers may also include some study and discussion of religious influences on literature. Shakespeare, for example, was nurtured on the Bible, and his writings are filled with biblical language and imagery.

More recently, English teachers have also begun studying religious works for their literary content. Thayer Warshaw, who pioneered this approach, observed that there is a long history of including some biblical passages in English courses. Until recently, however, he says that "what students were [usually] getting were really somewhat watered down, interdenominational, Protestant Sunday School lessons."[86]

---

86. Thayer S. Warshaw, quoted in "Blending Religion Into the Curriculum," *The New York Times*, April 15, 1984, Section XII, p. 51.

Today, many English teachers have adopted a more academic study of the Bible as literature. For example, "The Bible as Literature," a one-quarter elective course, is taught each year at Apollo High School in St. Cloud, Minnesota. During the course, students examine a variety of literary forms contained in the Bible, including poetry, short stories, parables, songs, drama, and letters. The course also includes comparisons of a variety of translations of the Bible and an examination of some of the biblical allusions throughout most of Western literature.

A third major curricular trend is helping students understand the relationships between civil government and religious liberty. Such an understanding is a critical part of preparing youth to live in a multi-faithed society.

The American Bar Association's Law-Related Education Program has found that a number of school districts are including some discussion of First Amendment issues in social studies classes. For example, 11th grade students in the Northport-East Northport Union Free School District may elect a year-long American history course called "American History Through Constitutional Law." In the unit on the First Amendment, students study landmark Supreme Court cases defining standards for the relationship between the schools and religion. They elect to play the role of either the petitioner or the respondent in one major case and present legal arguments before a mock Supreme Court.

School districts have adopted a number of other approaches to incorporating the study of religion into the public school curriculum. These approaches are units or courses that expose students to:
- the study of how religion and civilization developed
- the Bible as a classic for literary qualities
- the flag, the Constitution, and other American symbols that include religious dimensions
- Bible stories or Bible lands in literature and history
- legends in religions
- various religious movements in our present and past cultures
- comparative religious history
- religious institutions in the development of citizens for life in a society where people of various faiths must learn to live together
- 'various religions so that the student may determine his own personal philosophy, values, and relationship to various institutions.[87]

Obviously, the preparation of teachers is vital to the success of any

---

87. J.B. Morris, *The Instructional Status of Academic Religion in Large City Public High Schools in the United States* (unpublished Ed.D. dissertation, Baylor University, 1970), quoted in J.B. Morris, "Religion in the Public Schools," *The American School Board Journal*, December 1981, p. 47.

RESOURCES FOR TEACHING ABOUT RELIGIONS

School administrators may wish to plan an inservice course on teaching about religions. The National Council on Religion and Public Education, 1300 Oread, Lawrence, Kansas, or the Public Education Religion Studies Center, Wright State University, Dayton, Ohio 45435, can suggest consultants. A partial bibliography on teaching about religions follows:

Knicker, Charles. *Teaching About Religion in the Public Schools*, Series No. 224. Bloomington, Indiana: Phi Delta Kappa Educational Foundation, 1985.

Lines, Patricia M. *Religion and Moral Values in Public Schools: A Constitutional Analysis*. Denver, Colorado: Education Commission of the States, 1981.

Piedescalzi, Nicholas, and Collie, William (eds.). *Teaching About Religion in Public Schools*. Argus Communications, 1977.

Warshaw, Thayer. *Handbook for Teaching the Bible in Literature Classes*. Nashville: Abingdon Press, 1978. Also a nine-page supplement available from the author, 45 Clark Road, Andover, Massachusetts 01810.

Warshaw, Thayer. "Preparation for Teaching About Religions in Public Schools," *Religious Education*, Vol. 81, No. 1, Winter 1986, p. 79 ff.

Wood, James E. (ed). *Religion, the State, and Education*. Waco: Baylor University Press, 1984.

World Religions Curriculum Development Center, 6425 W. 33rd Street, Minneapolis, Minnesota 55426.

JOURNALS

Journal of Church and State, published three times per year. J.M. Dawson Studies in Church and State, Baylor University, Waco, Texas.

Religion & Public Education, published four times per year. National Council on Religion and Public Education, Lawrence, Kansas.

---

academic study of religions. The Public Education Religion Studies Center (PERSC) observed that, like all teachers, those who teach religion studies should be "professionally qualified, emotionally mature, and pedagogically sound."[88] In addition, PERSC suggested that those who teach about religions should also be "well-versed in the legal issues surrounding religion studies in public education, academically qualified in religion as an academic subject, and non-confessional in approach." It is particularly important that teachers dealing with religions in the classroom have an

---

88. James K. Uphoff, "Instructional Issues in Teaching About Religion, *Social Education*, January 1981, p. 23.

understanding of religious diversity and a belief in religious tolerance. The National Council for the Social Studies emphasizes that teachers must "equally value each and every student as worthy human beings regardless of race, sex, religion, ethnic origin, socio-economic level, or level of achievement."

The late Rabbi Samuel Sandmel, a professor, author, and chairman of the PERSC Professional Advisory Committee, suggested that many teachers can achieve the basic requirements for teaching religions:

> I do not think a high school teacher needs to have a Ph.D. in Scripture. I suppose the first thing is for a teacher to recognize the possible divergency of presuppositions among students. He or she needs some sense of responsibility, some awareness of his [or her] own disposition, some awareness of the diversity in class, and some sensitivity to the ways in which Scripture has been regarded.... He ought to have enough detachment to abstain from presenting his own view, whether it is intuitive or trained, as the only view. And if he undertakes to reflect views which he personally does not hold, then he should do so with fairness.[89]

Despite a renewed interest in teaching about religions, there are still relatively few schools that formally incorporate the subject into the curriculum. One reason may be a general decline in the number of elective courses. School districts that offer few elective courses may prefer to incorporate specific units on religions into other courses.

Other districts may avoid formal teaching about religions because of a fear that any mention of the subject may be a violation of the Supreme Court's rulings. On the contrary, the Court has indicated quite the opposite—as long as the study of religion is treated objectively and academically.

The state of Minnesota was concerned about finding constitutionally appropriate ways to include the study of religions in the curriculum. On the one hand, the state board of education wanted to make sure that public school students have a chance to learn about the important contributions that religions have made to human civilization. On the other hand, the board wanted to make sure that no student's belief—or nonbelief—was harmed in a public school.

The board appointed a broad-based task force, including among others, representatives of the American Civil Liberties Union, the Minnesota Catholic Conference, and a religious representative from one of

---

89. Samuel Sandmel, "Objectivity and Teaching the Bible," in Peter Bracher et al., eds. *Religion Studies in the Curriculum: Retrospect and Prospect, 1963-1983*, Dayton, Ohio: Public Education Religion Studies Center, Wright State University, 1974, pp. 48-50.

RECOMMENDATIONS FOR TEACHING ABOUT RELIGIONS

If your school district is concerned about appropriate ways to include teaching about religions in your school curriculum, here are some important considerations:

- The study of religions in public schools is permitted by the Constitution as long as the subject matter is presented objectively as part of a secular program of education.
- Teachers of religion courses should be sensitive to varying beliefs of their students.
- The First Amendment does not forbid all mention of religion in the public schools. It does prohibit the *advancement* or *inhibition* of religion.
- Public schools are not required to delete from their curriculum materials that may offend any religious sensibility.
- The decision to include—or exclude—material from the curriculum must be based on secular, not religious, reasons.
- The material must be presented objectively.
- Religion should be taught with the same care and discipline as other academic courses.
- Schools should be especially sensitive to the developmental differences between elementary and secondary school students. Subjects or teaching methods that may be appropriate for secondary students may not be appropriate for younger children.

Minnesota's Indian tribes. After considerable discussion, the task force developed a set of guidelines for all Minnesota public schools. Those guidelines could serve as a springboard for similar task forces in other school districts. (See page 34.)

In 1964, AASA's Commission on Religion in the Public Schools summarized the debate regarding religion in the curriculum by noting that "a curriculum that ignored religion would itself have serious religious implications. It would seem to proclaim that religion has not been as real in men's lives as health or politics or economics. By omission, it would appear to deny that religion has been and is important in human history—a denial of the obvious." And further, "In day by day practice, the topic of religion cannot be avoided. As an integral part of human culture, it must be included in the curriculum."

NATIONAL COUNCIL FOR THE SOCIAL STUDIES STATEMENT:

Knowledge about religions is not only a characteristic of an educated person but is also absolutely necessary for understanding and living in a world of diversity. Knowledge of religious differences and the role of religion in the contemporary world can help promote understanding and alleviate prejudice. Since the purpose of the social studies is to provide students with a knowledge of the world that has been, the world that is, and the world of the future, studying about religions should be an essential part of the social studies curriculum. Omitting study about religions gives students the impression that religions have not been and are not now part of the human experience. Study about religions may be dealt with in special courses and units or whatever and whenever knowledge of the religious dimension of human history and culture is needed for a balanced and comprehensive understanding.

—taken from position statement and guidelines governing study
about religions in the social studies curriculum,
adopted by the plenum of the National Council for the Social Studies, 1984

GUIDELINES FOR TEACHING ABOUT RELIGIONS

1. The school may sponsor the *study* of religion, but may not sponsor the *practice* of religion.
2. The school may *expose* students to all religious views, but may not *impose* any particular view.
3. The school's approach to religion is one of *instruction*, not one of *indoctrination*.
4. The function of the school is to *educate* about all religions, not to *convert* to any one religion.
5. The school's approach is *academic*, not *devotional*.
6. The school should *study* what all people believe, but should not *teach* a student what to believe.
7. The school should strive for student *awareness* of all religions, but should not press for student *acceptance* of any one religion.
8. The school should seek to *inform* the student about various beliefs, but should not seek to *conform* him or her to any one belief.

—from "Public Education Religion Studies: Questions and Answers,"
Public Education Religion Studies Center,
Wright State University, Dayton, Ohio, 1974.

STATE OF MINNESOTA
POLICY ON TEACHING ABOUT RELIGIONS IN THE PUBLIC SCHOOLS

RECOMMENDATIONS FOR RESOLVING RELIGIOUSLY SENSITIVE ISSUES

Customs, Practices and Policies that may *not* be permitted include:

1. Schools may not incorporate into their sponsored programs religious worship or indoctrination.
2. School programs may not provide for compulsory reading from the Bible as part of a non-instructional activity.
3. Schools may not promote or indoctrinate any religion including theism, atheism, agnosticism, humanism, secularism, sectarianism, yoga, transcendental meditation.
4. School officials may not compose, authorize, or sanction prayers.
5. Sectarian instruction may not be offered to students in public schools during school hours.
6. Sectarian instruction may not be offered in any school sponsored activity.
7. Official public school musical groups may not participate under the auspices of the public school in religious services.
8. Non-student members of religious groups are not allowed in the school to proselytize or recruit during the school day or during school activities.
9. Official posting or display of religious documents such as the Ten Commandments and other religious symbols except when related to the curriculum is not considered appropriate.
10. Celebration of religious Holy Days and the fostering of a religious spirit is inappropriate in the schools.
11. Public schools should not facilitate/allow the distribution of sectarian literature, including Bibles and religious tracts, in the schools by school staff and non-school persons, unless directly related to the approved curriculum.

Customs, practices, and policies that *may* be permitted include:

1. Schools may use the Bible or other religious books as source books in teaching about religions.
2. Schools should recognize the multiplicity of explanations related to human origins in their appropriate curricular place.
3. A student has the right to pray at any appropriate time.

4. Schools may offer objective instruction about religion as literature and history and religion's role in the story of civilization.
5. Schools are free to recite such documents as the Declaration of Independence which contain references to God.
6. Students may sing the national anthem and other patriotic songs which contain assertions of faith in God.
7. Rhetorical or personal references to religious faith in connection with patriotic or ceremonial occasions are permissible.
8. Students may be dismissed for sectarian instruction off school premises. (See Minnesota Statutes sec. 120.10, Subc. 3.)
9. Schools may excuse a student from engaging in an activity which offends that student's religious belief or conscience.
10. Classroom instruction, where its content is in the area of religious Holy Days or celebrations, should be carefully tied to educational objectives. These educational objectives should be specified in writing and consistent with the overall curriculum of the school.
11. The school calendar, vacations and holidays may be scheduled to permit observances of religious Holy Days. When school is scheduled on a religious Holy Day, students shall be excused for observance of the Holy Day upon the request of their parents.

THE PLACE OF RELIGIOUSLY SENSITIVE MATERIAL IN THE CURRICULUM

CREATIONISM

The previous section emphasized the difference between *teaching* religion and teaching *about* religions. The recent debate over "creationism" offers an example of a controversy that arises when public schools are asked to teach religion (which is not permitted by the Constitution).

Members of some religious groups, particularly Christian fundamentalists who believe in a literal interpretation of the Bible's "Book of Genesis," have tried to pass laws or develop school district policies that would prohibit the teaching of Darwinian theory. Others have tried to require teachers who do discuss Darwinian theory also to teach the "creationist" theory, which holds that the Book of Genesis provides the only acceptable explanation of how the world was created.

One of the earliest legislative attempts to require schools to teach creationism was a 1928 Arkansas statute making it unlawful for any teacher in any state-supported school or university "to teach the theory or doctrine that mankind ascended or descended from a lower order of animals," or "to adopt or use in any such institution a textbook that teaches this theory."[90] Violators of the law were subject to dismissal. It continued in effect long after other states had abandoned such laws because of the celebrated *Scopes* trial.

In 1965, Susan Epperson, a high school biology teacher in Little Rock, received a new set of textbooks, selected through the school district's official textbook selection process. These new textbooks included a chapter on the Darwinian theory.

Mrs. Epperson first tried to get the state's supreme court to declare the statute void, but the state court held that the law was a valid expression of the state's power to specify curriculum for its public schools. Mrs. Epperson taught the prohibited chapter and was dismissed from her job.

On appeal the U.S. Supreme Court declared the Arkansas law unconstitutional. Justice Fortas, writing for the Court, noted

> The overriding fact is that Arkansas' law selects from the body of knowledge a particular segment which it proscribes for the sole reason that it is deemed to conflict with a particular religious doctrine; that is, with a particular interpretation of the Book of Genesis by a particular group. . . .[91]
>
> There is and can be no doubt that the First Amendment does not permit the State to require that teaching and learning must be tailored to the principles or prohibitions of any religious sect or dogma. . . .[92]
>
> Arkansas has sought to prevent its teachers from discussing the theory of evolution because it is contrary to the belief of some that the Book of Genesis must be the exclusive source of doctrine as to the origin of man. No suggestion has been made that Arkansas' law may be justified by considerations of state policy other than the religious views of some of its citizens.[93]

In other words, the Court held that it is unconstitutional for school districts to remove a particular subject from the curriculum primarily *to accommodate the religious views of a particular group of citizens*. However, the Court also implied that school authorities have other grounds for removing subject matter from the curriculum. For example, in a concurring opinion, Justice Black said: "[T]here is no reason. . . why a State is without power to withdraw from its curriculum any subject deemed too emotion-

---

90. *Epperson v. Arkansas*, 393 U.S. 97, 98-99 (1968).
91. *Ibid.*, at 103.
92. *Ibid.*, at 106.
93. *Ibid.*, at 107.

al and controversial for its public schools."[94] In most cases, the Court concluded, the control of local educational policy should be left to state and local authorities.

The Supreme Court has to date ruled only on the question of excluding certain material from the curriculum primarily on religious grounds.[95] However, there have been lower court decisions that have discussed the question of *including* the creationist theory in the curriculum.

For example, legislatures in Tennessee, Arkansas, and Louisiana all passed "Balanced Treatment" laws, requiring science textbooks that treated the subject of evolution also to treat equally the creationist theory. All these laws have been found unconstitutional on the grounds that they promote a particular religious view. For example, in Arkansas,[96] court testimony revealed that the author of the bill, who described himself as a born-again Christian, knew that the law would require schools to teach religious doctrine. The Arkansas law was thus held impermissible because the court found it had a clearly religious purpose.

However, Patricia Lines, an authority on the First Amendment and the schools, suggests that it may be possible to develop a constitutionally valid policy regarding the teaching of creationism. This teaching method would satisfy "those who seek to include [creationism in the curriculum] for strictly educational reasons."[97]

Lines suggests that religiously sensitive material, such as the creationist theory, may constitutionally be included in the curriculum if it is subject to the same kind of critical inquiry that any other scientific theory receives. "If, as creationists maintain, creationist theory deserves inclusion in science classes for intellectual reasons, then it too must be verified by conventional scientific methods."[98]

Creationism, however, is based on the literal interpretation of the Book of Genesis. In fact, members of the Creation Research Society sign a statement that reads, 'The Bible is the Written Word of God, and because it is inspired thruout [sic], all its assertions are historically and scientifically true.... To the student of nature this means that the account of origins in Genesis is a factual presentation of simple historical truth."[99]

This conflict creates a dilemma for educators. As Lines points out, including the creationist theory in the curriculum but subjecting it to

---

94. *Ibid.*, at 113.
95. The Court will hear a case regarding a challenge to the Louisiana law in its 1986-87 session.
96. *McLean v. Arkansas Board of Education*, 529 F.Supp. 1255 (E.D. Ark. 1982).
97. Patricia Lines, "Scientific Creationism in the Classroom: A Constitutional Dilemma," *Loyola Law Review*, XXVIII, 1982, reprinted in *NCRPE Bulletin*, Vol. 10, No. 3, Summer 1983, p. 36.
98. *Ibid.*
99. *McLean v. Arkansas Board of Education*, 529 F.Supp. 1255, n. 7 at 1260 (1982).

critical inquiry—which she calls "the only constitutionally valid way such a demand can be met"—may in fact "jeopardize the belief of children imbued with fundamentalist principles."[100]

How can schools accommodate the religious beliefs of students who believe in the creationist theory of the world's origin? One way may be to excuse students from part or all of a course in which Darwinian theory of evolution is taught. Lines even suggests that classes such as biology might be organized in modular units, which would permit students to opt out of particular course segments without being singled out by their peers. (See Section on "Excusal" for other guidelines on excusal.)

"SECULAR HUMANISM"

The emotional charge that schools are teaching the "religion" of "secular humanism" offers one of the clearest illustrations of the tension between the Establishment Clause and the Free Exercise Clause of the First Amendment. The statement is usually made by those who oppose the Supreme Court's rulings that have removed religious practices such as prayer, "scientific creationism," and Bible reading from the public schools.

Rather than removing the influence of religion from the schools, some conservative fundamentalists argue, the schools have instead installed a secular religion, called secular humanism. The argument says that unless school administrators allow religious practices in schools, they are themselves participating in an unconstitutional establishment of a religion—the religion of secular humanism.

Definitions of secular humanism vary. One definition frequently used by the Religious Right comes from Mel and Norma Gabler through their firm, Educational Research Analysts:

> Humanism is faith in man instead of faith in God. Humanism was officially ruled a religion by the U.S. Supreme Court. Humanism promotes: (1) situational ethics, (2) evolution, (3) sexual freedom, including public sex education courses, and (4) internationalism.[101]

In fact, the Supreme Court has twice referred to secular humanism as a religion, once in a footnote that says, "Among religions in this country which do not teach what would generally be considered a belief in the existence of God are Buddhism, Taoism, Ethical Culture, Secular Human-

---

100. Lines, p. 36.
101. Printed sheet entitled "The Mel Gablers' Educational Research Analysts," November 1977, quoted in Edward Jenkinson, "Schoolbook Skirmishes Leave Longlasting Scars," *Religion & Public Education*, Vol. 13, No. 1, Winter 1986, p. 24.

ism, and others,"[102] and a second time in a footnote referring to the first case.[103]

As the Gablers' own definition indicates, the phrase "secular humanism" varies from speaker to speaker. One observer has called it, "a slogan without precise definition."[104] For example, religious and other groups trying to remove one subject or another from the public schools have cited the following practices and content as examples of secular humanism: drug education, death education, values clarification, global education, the study of socialism, the theory of evolution, and the look-say method of reading.

Some school critics disagree among themselves over what "secular humanism" means. But they are united in their disagreement with the Court's interpretation of the First Amendment. As Chapter II emphasized, the First Amendment's Establishment Clause requires that schools remain *neutral* on the subject of religion. That means that no religious group can use the schools to espouse its own interests.

Some school critics disagree with this philosophy of neutrality. The judge who found an Arkansas law requiring that schools teach both creationism and the evolutionary theory unconstitutional says that he received one letter that said, "public schools ought to teach religion—my kind."[105]

One conservative columnist says that the "gripe" of conservative parents is that "their children, in their public schools, are being denied their First Amendment rights to exercise their religious faith."[106] And it seems likely that questions of free exercise—not establishment—may be the real cause of the debate over secular humanism.

Those who levy the charge of secular humanism against the schools often cite as evidence the fact that John Dewey signed *Humanist Manifesto I* in 1933 and B.F. Skinner signed *Humanist Manifesto II* in 1973. Since these two noted educators signed documents professing their belief in humanism, some argue, all educators therefore subscribe to the philosophy presented in the documents.

There are, of course, several fallacies in the argument. One of the most obvious is the logical fallacy of stating that because one or two influential educators call themselves secular humanists, all other educators must also be humanists. Statements that all educators are secular human-

---

102. *Torcasco v. Watkins*, 367 U.S. 488, n. 11 at 495 (1961).
103. Jenkinson, p. 26.
104. John Swomley, p. 21.
105. Overton, p. 24.
106. John Lofton, "They May Regret Ever Raising the Issue," *The Washington Times*, March 10, 1986.

ists are simply inaccurate, and greatly underestimate the professionalism and dedication of American educators.

In fact, nearly 80 percent of American educators are members of a church or synagogue, and approximately 60 percent say they attend religious services almost every week.[107] On the job, however, educators make conscientious attempts *not* to impose their beliefs on students. If individual teachers or administrators do use the classroom to espouse their personal beliefs, whether those beliefs are Christianity, Judaism, any other religious philosophy, or secular humanism, they are violating the Constitution. Such cases should be dealt with directly. However, most teachers and administrators take their obligation to uphold the Constitution in the schools very seriously.

CENSORSHIP

Accusations of secular humanism are one example of the growing number of attempts to censor what is available to teach in schools. During the 1984-85 school year, there were attempts in 46 states to remove certain material from classrooms or school library shelves.[108] Not all these censorship attempts came from conservative parents—for example, one school board rejected a Latin American history textbook they found to be "anti-Soviet."[109]

In general, courts have tended to give local school districts wide discretion in determining what they teach. In the *Epperson* case, discussed in Chapter II, the Supreme Court noted:

Public education in our Nation is committed to the control of state and local authorities. Courts do not and cannot intervene in the resolution of conflicts which arise in the daily operation of school systems and which do not directly and sharply implicate basic constitutional values.[110]

At the same time, however, the Court has frequently upheld the overriding importance of preserving freedom of speech. In one case, the Court went so far as to say that "the classroom is peculiarly the 'marketplace of ideas.' "[111] The Court has also stated its belief that "the First Amendment... does not tolerate laws which cast a pall of orthodoxy over the classroom."[112]

---

107. C. Emily Feistritzer, *Profiles of Teachers in the United States,* National Center for Education Information, 1986, p. 58. A major National Education Association survey of teachers found that more than 77.5 percent listed themselves as members of a church or synagogue.
108. Barbara Parker, "Stop the Censors," *New York Times,* August 29, 1985, Sec. I, p. 23.
109. *Ibid.*
110. *Epperson v. Arkansas,* 393 U.S. 97, 104 (1968).
111. *Keyishian v. Board of Regents,* 385 U.S. 589, 603 (1976).
112. *Ibid.,* at 683.

When school districts establish a comprehensive set of standards for selecting materials for the classroom or the library, and then follow a written set of procedures for evaluating materials against those standards, they are likely to have those policies upheld in case of a court challenge. The Sarasota, Florida, school district, for example, has developed written standards governing the inclusion of materials in schools dealing with religion, ideologies, sex, and profanity in schools. The district also uses a standard form for any parent requesting reconsideration of any instructional material. (See box, page 42.)

How can school districts provide a peaceful way for parents to challenge books and ideas that are included in the curriculum while guaranteeing that the schools will reflect a diversity of opinion? Edward Jenkinson, professor of education at Indiana University, has examined censorship controversies across the United States. He has found that many of these controversies leave "long-lasting scars and, in many cases, wounds that will never heal." His suggestions for reducing the conflict include the following steps as a minimum:

1. Review the selection policies for classroom and library materials to make certain that the policies are comprehensive and that they make it possible for teachers to introduce a variety of ideas, facts, and literature in the classroom. The policies should also insure that school libraries can actually be a [resource] for a wide range of materials—both controversial and innocuous.

2. Review the procedures for handling complaints against teaching materials. Make certain that the procedures do not give anyone the authority to remove a book without the full action and recommendation of a duly authorized reconsideration committee. Also, make certain that the procedures call for that very important, informal first step in which the person lodging the complaint has the opportunity to talk with the person—librarian or teacher—responsible for the "objectionable" work.

3. Make certain that the school system has adequately informed citizens of its educational philosophy, of its curriculum, of its goals and objectives, of its policies and procedures.

4. Make certain that anyone who has a complaint about a book, a film, a teaching method, or whatever, is given a fair hearing.

5. Insist on a public hearing when a citizen demands that a book be removed from a classroom or library.

6. Form support groups of parents and other members of the community who want to maintain the First Amendment rights of students and teachers and who will resist censorship. School systems that have organized such informal support groups have discovered that some clergy are willing to become active members of such groups.

7. Study attempts to censor school materials to learn the targets and tactics of the schoolbook protesters. Learn their buzz words and be prepared to refute their charges.

8. Be prepared to... refute unfounded charges about classroom activities and the school system's alleged indoctrination of students in the religion of secular humanism.

9. Do the best job possible.[113]

POLICY FOR USE IN THE SELECTION OF EDUCATIONAL MEDIA, SARASOTA SCHOOL DISTRICT, SARASOTA, FLORIDA

Three types of materials are sometimes topics of criticism. Criteria for including these materials for school use are listed below:

1. *Religion*— Factual unbiased materials which represent all major religions shall be included in the Media Center collections.
2. *Ideologies*— The Media Center shall, without making any effort to sway reader judgment, make available basic factual information on the school level, on any ideology or philosophy which exerts a strong force, either favorably or unfavorably in government, current events, politics, education, or any other phase of life.
3. *Sex and Profanity*— Materials presenting accents on sex shall be subject to a stern test of literary merit and reality by the professional staff who take into consideration the school level and accepted public moral standards. While the sensational or overdramatic should never be included, the fact of sexual incidents or profanity appearing shall not automatically disqualify a book. Rather the decision shall be made on the basis of whether the book is of literary value. Factual materials of any educational nature on the school level shall be included in the Media Center collection.

If your school district is faced with a decision of whether to include—or exclude—religiously sensitive material in the curriculum, here are some issues you need to consider.
- What is the *purpose* of including or excluding the material in the curriculum? The *Epperson* decision prohibits eliminating any materials from the curriculum because of religious objections. The same

---
113. Jenkinson, p. 27.

reasoning can be applied to material that is *included* exclusively for religious reasons.
- The decision to include—or exclude—material from the curriculum must be based on secular, not religious, reasons.
- What approach will be used in discussing the material? For example, will the creationist theory in a science course be subjected to the same kind of critical evaluation and discussion as the Darwinian theory?
- Educational policymakers have "no legitimate interest in protecting any or all religions from views distasteful to them," according to the *Burstyn* decision.[114]
- The Supreme Court has repeatedly held that "the First Amendment... does not tolerate laws which cast a pall of orthodoxy over the classroom."[115]

EXCUSAL

As Chapter II pointed out, courts have at times approved laws or regulations that allowed individuals to be *excused* from the application of a particular law or regulation in view of their religious beliefs. Students have been excused from saluting the flag and even—in the *Yoder* case—from attending high school altogether when they have been able to prove that such actions violate their right to free exercise of religion.

Courts have repeatedly upheld policies that permit students to be excused from portions of the curriculum on religious grounds. In Illinois, students who were members of the United Pentecostal Church objected to coeducational physical education classes because they considered the typical dress of other students to be "immodest." A lower court permitted the students to be excused from the class.[116] However, Vermont students who asked to be excused from physical education class on the nonreligious grounds of modesty and dislike for competitive athletics were not permitted to be excused.[117]

Of course, if a school policy violates the First Amendment's Establishment Clause by advancing religion, the fact that schools excuse students who object to participating in the activity will not make an otherwise unconstitutional policy permissible. For example, the Supreme

---

114. 343 U.S. 495, 505 (1952).
115. *Keyishian v. Board of Regents*, 385 U.S. 589, 603 (1967).
116. *Moody v. Cronin*, 484 F.Supp. 270 (C.D. Ill. 1979), cited in Patricia Lines, *Religious and Moral Values in Public Schools: A Constitutional Analysis*, Law and Education Center, Education Commission of the States, 1981, p. 41.
117. *Ouimette v. Babbie*, 405 F.Supp. 525 (D. Vt. 1975), cited in Lines, *Ibid.*

THE SCHOOL BOARD OF SARASOTA COUNTY, FLORIDA, PATRON'S REQUEST FOR RECONSIDERATION OF INSTRUCTIONAL MATERIAL

Author: _____ Book: _____ Film: _____ Other: _____
Title: _____
Publisher or Producer (if known): _____
Location of Material (i.e., school): _____
Request initiated by: _____ Date: _____
Telephone: _____
Address: _____
City: _____ State: _____ Zip: _____
Complainant represents
_____ himself
_____ (name organization) _____
_____ (identify other group) _____

* (If objection is to material other than a book or film, change wording of the following questions so that they apply. Please use back of form if you need more space.)

1. To what in the material do you object? Please be specific, cite pages or segments.
2. What do you feel might be the result of exposure to this material?
3. For what age group would you recommend this material?
4. Are there any desirable features about the material?
5. Did you read or see the entire book or film? What parts?
6. Are you aware of the judgment of this material by recognized critics?
7. What do you believe is the theme of this material?
8. What would you like done with this material?
   _____ do not assign/lend or expose it to my child.
   _____ withdraw it from all students as well as my child.
   _____ send it back to the staff selection personnel for re-evaluation.
9. In its place, what material of equal quality would you recommend that would convey as valuable a picture and perspective of our civilization and the subject treated?

Court ruled in *Engel v. Vitale*[118] and more recently in *Wallace v. Jaffree*[119] that required prayer in schools is unconstitutional even if students who

---
118. 370 U.S. 421 (1962).
119. 105 S.Ct. 2479 (1985).

> ## SHAKER HEIGHTS, OHIO, SCHOOL DISTRICT POLICY ON RELIGIOUS HOLIDAYS
>
> Religious education is the responsibility of the home, church, and temple and within the schools will remain the free choice of the individual true to the American heritage and Constitution.
>
> Religious neutrality is not only mandated by the Constitution, it is also sound educational policy. Introduction of religious observances, devotions, or celebrations into the schools can only serve to make some children uncomfortable. Religious celebrations often force children to choose between participating in the celebration or isolating themselves from their classmates by not participating. The U.S. Supreme Court has long recognized the great pressure on children to conform with their peers. Accordingly, schools should avoid practices which operate to single out and isolate the "different" pupils and thereby serve to embarrass and harass those children who wish to be excused. . . .
>
> Teachers may explain the meanings of religious holidays provided every effort is made to obtain adequate and authentic information on matters pertaining to religion. *Teachers should avoid the potential embarrassment of asking students to explain their own religious practices or observances, or to bring religious objects to class as a basis for a discussion of holiday observances.* . . .
>
> A pupil's absence from school on a religious holiday should be recognized as an excused absence, without penalty on scholastic or attendance records. So as not to penalize students for their religious observance, the scheduling of examinations, assemblies, field trips, graduation exercises, and other special events, including school-related programs for parents, should be avoided on religious holidays.
>
> —Shaker Heights City School District,
> Shaker Heights, Ohio
> Adopted 1980 [emphasis added]

object are permitted to be excused.

Furthermore, the Court has recognized that for most students, the desire to fit in with their peers and avoid harassment may exert pressure on them to conform. Justice Frankfurter once observed that for most students, "The law of imitation operates, and non-conformity is not an outstanding characteristic of children."[120] In general, schools should not rely on excusal as their primary way of accommodating students' reli-

---

120. *McCollum v. Board of Education*, 333 U.S. 203, 227 (1948).

gious views. The Shaker Heights, Ohio, school district has adopted a policy that addresses this subject directly (printed on page 45).

Nevertheless, excusal can be a valid way for school administrators to accommodate the free exercise of a diversity of religious beliefs. For example, some students may need to be excused from portions of science classes in which evolution is taught if it violates their religious beliefs.[121] In the *Yoder* case, however, the Court made clear that school districts need not excuse students if doing so would defeat an important educational goal.

Students may also need to be excused from school to participate in religious observances. The Associated Press, for example, reported that the Dade County, Florida, schools excused a third-grader's absence from school for several weeks as she underwent ceremonies for becoming a priestess in the ancient African Santeria religion.[122]

Most school districts also grant religious leave to teachers. The Fairfax County, Virginia, schools, for example, grant two days leave to employees for "religious holidays in cases where observance prevents the employee from working." The district policy adds that "leave will be granted unless it has a severe impact on the instructional program." In a 1985 case, however, the Supreme Court ruled that employees do not have an absolute right to be excused from work on their Sabbath.

If your school district is considering a policy of excusal for religiously sensitive subject matter, here are some considerations to keep in mind:

- School districts are required to excuse students from studies or assignments that conflict with the free exercise of their religion.
- Excusing students from participating in a specific activity will not permit school districts to adopt policies that would otherwise violate the Establishment Clause.
- Whenever possible, school calendars should be developed so that major school activities do not conflict with important religious holidays. The National Conference of Christians and Jews publishes a calendar that lists major holidays of the Baha'i, Buddhist, Christian, Hindu, Muslim, Jewish, and Sikh faiths. (The calendar is available free of charge.)[123]
- A student's absence from school for religious reasons should be recognized as an excused absence.

---

121. Lines, p. 41.
122. Associated Press, December 8, 1984.
123. National Conference of Christians and Jews, 71 Fifth Avenue, New York, New York, 10003.

CHAPTER IV

RELIGION AND NONCURRICULAR POLICIES OF PUBLIC SCHOOLS

The interaction between the public schools and religions extends beyond what is taught in the classroom. It also includes a number of other sensitive issues. Should any religious holidays be recognized in the public schools; and, if so, in what manner should they be recognized? What about other religious practices, such as posting the Ten Commandments or sponsoring baccalaureate services? May school districts provide instructional aid to religious schools? Finally, are there ways that schools and religious groups can work together to improve education? This chapter deals with each of these topics.

RELIGIOUS HOLIDAYS

Many school districts share the educational goal of advancing students' knowledge of and appreciation for the role of our nation's religious heritage. And because, as Justice William O. Douglas observed in *Zorach v. Clauson*, "We are a religious people whose institutions presuppose a Supreme Being,"[124] many religious holidays have also come to have a secular importance in American life.

The question of how best to acknowledge holidays in the public schools has presented school administrators and teachers with a particular challenge. Is it possible to recognize religious holidays in the schools with-

---

124. 343 U.S. 306, 313 (1952).

out violating either the Establishment Clause or the Free Exercise Clause of the First Amendment?

The question of holiday observances in schools may be considered as either a curricular or a noncurricular issue. However, since the most emotional arguments usually revolve around Christmas programs, we have included the discussion in this chapter.

There have been no Supreme Court rulings on this subject. However, one school district's policies governing holiday recognition have been reviewed and upheld by the Eighth Circuit Court of Appeals. This case suggests some of the important issues school administrators must consider when formulating a policy for their schools.

Schools in the Sioux Falls, South Dakota, school district had presented a variety of assemblies during the Christmas holiday season for many years. In 1977, two kindergarten classes rehearsed, memorized, and performed a Christmas assembly that included the following "Beginners Christmas Quiz":

Teacher: Of whom did heav'nly angels sing
              And news about His birthday bring?
Class: Jesus.
Teacher: Now, can you name the little town
              Where they the Baby Jesus found?
Class: Bethlehem.
Teacher: Where had they made a little bed
              For Christ, the blessed Saviour's head?
Class: In a manger in a cattle stall.
Teacher: What is the day we celebrate
              As birthday of this One so great?
Class: Christmas. [125]

Roger L. Florey, a parent of one of the kindergarteners, complained that this poem actually constituted a religious observance in the public schools. In response to this complaint and several others, the school district established a committee to study how the schools could most appropriately deal with religion-state issues. The committee included parents, teachers, an attorney, a member of the American Civil Liberties Union, and the school district's music supervisor, as well as Protestant, Catholic, and Jewish clergy. After months of study by the committee and after public hearings on the subject, the school board adopted a new set of policy guidelines governing the school district's recognition of religious beliefs and customs and recognition of religious holidays in the public schools. Those guidelines are reprinted on page 51.

---

125. *Florey v. Sioux Falls School District,* 464 F.Supp. 911, 192, (1979).

Mr. Florey and others filed suit to prevent the guidelines from being implemented, charging that they violated the Establishment Clause of the First Amendment. Both the federal district court and the Eighth Circuit Court of Appeals upheld the school district's policy. Both courts found that the policy did not violate any of the tests established in *Lemon v. Kurtzman*.

For example, the courts noted that the citizens' committee was originally established as a way to ensure that no religious exercise was a part of school-sponsored activities. In addition, the Sioux Falls school district's rules did not require any school to sponsor holiday activities. Their purpose was only to allow certain programs to be included in the curriculum if the teachers felt that they would make appropriate educational sense.

The courts also held that the *effect* of the rules was neither to advance nor to inhibit religion. Citing the *Nyquist* case,[126] the federal circuit court wrote that, "The First Amendment does not forbid all mention of religion in public schools; it is the *advancement* or *inhibition* of religion that is prohibited."

The circuit court noted that the study of religions had been approved in such Supreme Court cases as *Everson*, then added:

> We view the term "study" to include more than mere classroom instruction; public performance may be a legitimate part of secular study. This does not mean, of course, that religious ceremonies can be performed in the public schools under the guise of "study." It does mean, however, that when the primary purpose served by a given school activity is secular, that activity is not made unconstitutional by the inclusion of some religious content.[127]

Both the district court and the circuit court of appeals found that memorizing and performing the "Christmas Quiz" was primarily a religious activity. The citizens' committee, the school district, and the courts agreed that such a program would not be permitted under the new guidelines.

Nonetheless, this case suggests that some accommodation to religion is possible in the public schools, if the *purpose* of including the material is secular, and if the material is presented objectively.

This does not mean that school districts or individual schools are required to engage in holiday recognition. They may still opt for a stricter and less ambiguous interpretation of the Establishment Clause (compare, for example, the Shaker Heights, Ohio, district policy reprinted in

---

126. 413 U.S. 756, 788 (1973).
127. *Florey v. Sioux Falls School District*, 619 F.2d 1311, 1316 (1980).

Chapter III). But if teachers and administrators feel that some recognition of religious holidays is a part of the school's secular curriculum, it is possible to develop a district policy that will likely meet Constitutional standards.

If your school district is considering a policy on the recognition of religious holidays in the schools, here are some important considerations:
- The *purpose* of your school district policy should be based on academic reasons. Your policy is likely to be constitutionally sound if your goal is to promote the study and performance of a wide variety of music, for example, while ensuring that the schools do not sponsor religious activities. A goal like "putting Christ and Christmas back in the schools" is unlikely to pass constitutional tests. The purpose should be to inform students so they will understand the origin, history and meaning of the holidays to those who observe them.
- Administering of religious training is properly in the domain of the family and the religious institution. The First Amendment prohibits public schools from serving such a function.
- In general, your policy should ensure that schools recognize holidays that have both a religious and an educational basis.
- If your school district's goal is to permit students to recognize a number of religious holidays, then your *practice* must carry out that goal. If such a policy is in effect only once a year—during the Christmas season, for example—it is likely that its purpose will be carefully scrutinized and misunderstood.
- Students should never be required to participate in any activity that opposes their religious or nonreligious beliefs. However, *excusing students from such participation does not mean that your policy will not violate the Establishment Clause.*

OTHER RELIGIOUS PRACTICES

School districts may also need to consider policies governing other religious practices. For example, districts may be asked to display or distribute religious texts. One Supreme Court case, *Stone v. Graham*,[128] grew out of a Kentucky law that required schools to post a copy of the Ten Commandments in each classroom. Private funds were used to purchase the copies.

In a brief opinion, the Supreme Court found that the *purpose* of the law was the advancement of religion, and noted:

> This is not a case in which the Ten Commandments are integrated into the school curriculum, where the Bible may con-

---

128. 449 U.S. 39 (1980).

stitutionally be used in an appropriate study of history, civilization, ethics, comparative religion, or the like. . . .Posting of religious texts on the wall serves no such educational function.[129]

School baccalaureate services have never been reviewed by the Supreme Court. Nonetheless, the preceding cases should offer some idea about likely Supreme Court rulings on these services.

A baccalaureate service is a religious exercise. For that reason alone, baccalaureate services sponsored by school districts are likely to be found to violate the Establishment Clause.

Some school districts have adopted alternative policies to replace baccalaureate services. For example, in some communities a group of religious institutions may sponsor a religious service for all seniors who wish to attend. In other communities, students are encouraged to wear their graduation gowns when they attend religious services during graduation week. Another school district featured a "secular baccalaureate," in which students reflected on the individuals and ideas that had shaped their education.

SIOUX FALLS SCHOOL DISTRICT POLICY ON RELIGIOUS BELIEFS AND CUSTOMS AND ON OBSERVANCE OF RELIGIOUS HOLIDAYS

RECOGNITION OF RELIGIOUS BELIEFS AND CUSTOMS

It is accepted that no religious belief or non-belief should be promoted by the school district or its employees, and none should be disparaged. Instead, the school district should encourage all students and staff members to appreciate and be tolerant of religious views. The school district should use the opportunity to foster understanding and mutual respect among students and parents, whether it involves race, culture, economic background or religious beliefs. In that spirit of tolerance, students and staff members should be excused from participating in practices which are contrary to their religious beliefs, unless there are clear issues of overriding concern that would prevent it.

The Sioux Falls School District recognizes that one of its educational goals is to advance the student's knowledge and appreciation of the role that our religious heritage has played in the social, cultural, and historical development of civilization.

---

129. *Ibid.*, at 42.

OBSERVANCE OF RELIGIOUS HOLIDAYS

The practice of the Sioux Falls School District shall be as follows:

1. The several holidays throughout the year which have a religious and a secular basis may be observed in the public schools.
2. The historical and contemporary values and the origin of religious holidays may be explained in an unbiased and objective manner without sectarian indoctrination.
3. Music, art, literature and drama having religious themes or basis are permitted as part of the curriculum for school-sponsored activities and programs if presented in a prudent and objective manner and as a traditional part of the cultural and religious heritage of the particular holiday.
4. The use of religious symbols such as a cross, menorah, crescent, Star of David, creche, symbols of Native American religions or other symbols that are a part of a religious holiday are permitted as a teaching aid or resource provided such symbols are displayed as an example of the cultural and religious heritage of the holiday and are temporary in nature. Among these holidays are Christmas, Easter, Passover, Hannukah, St. Valentine's Day, St. Patrick's Day, Thanksgiving, and Halloween.
5. The school district's calendar should be prepared so as to minimize conflicts with religious holidays of all faiths.

However, participation by a clergyman at the opening or closing of a public program such as graduation cannot necessarily be considered an unconstitutional violation of the Establishment Clause. The Supreme Court has upheld the practice of opening every session of Congress with a prayer, and has noted that each Court session begins with the words "God save the United States and this Honorable Court."[130]

If your school district is evaluating policies about other religious practices in the schools, here are some issues to consider:

- Of the three-part test identified in *Lemon v. Kurzman*, the most prominent in finding practices unconstitutional seems to be *purpose*. If the purpose of the practice is to promote a religion, or all religions, it will be difficult for a court to uphold your district's practice.
- On these and other constitutional questions, it is always wise to consult an attorney who has experience in constitutional law, preferably the state attorney general.

---

130. *Zorach v. Clauson*, 343 U.S. 306, 313 (1952).

EXTRACURRICULAR BIBLE STUDY GROUPS OR CLUBS

For several years, student groups across the country have tried to gain school district permission to conduct student-led prayer or Bible study groups on school premises. In 1984, Congress passed the "Equal Access Act,"[131] designed to guarantee secondary school students the right to organize such meetings under certain limited circumstances.

There are three basic precepts that underly the passage of the Equal Access Act.

The first basic precept is equal treatment. If a public secondary school permits student groups to meet for student-initiated activity not related to the school curriculum, it is required to treat all such student groups equally. This means the school cannot discriminate against any students conducting such meetings "on the basis of the religious, political, philosophical, or other content of the speech at such meetings."[132] This language makes clear that religious speech should receive equal, but not preferred treatment.

The act specifies, however, that student-initiated meetings are permissible only in schools that provide what is called a "limited open forum"—an opportunity during noninstructional time for students to organize meetings and discuss subject matter not related to the school curriculum. If only curriculum-related groups, such as the debate club, the Latin club, student government, or athletic teams are permitted to meet in the school, no limited open forum exists.

The second basic precept is protection of student-initiated and student-led meetings. The Supreme Court has held unconstitutional state-initiated and state-sponsored religious activities.

Moreover, the act specifies that the meetings must not be led by adults; i.e., a monitor teacher must be present to see that order is maintained but may not participate. Further, "outside" adults may visit on occasion, but not regularly and not to conduct the meeting.

The Court has not yet ruled on the constitutionality of student-led meetings. The Court dismissed a case dealing with the constitutionality of extracurricular prayer meetings in Williamsport, Pennsylvania, only because the appeal had been made by a single member of the school board, who did not have the authority to appeal on his own.

A third precept underlying the act is the importance of local control of education. School administrators are permitted to establish regulations governing the time, place, and manner in which any "limited open

---

131. P.L. 98-377.
132. Sec. 802(a).

forum" will operate. For example, the school might decide that meetings could be held at a certain hour or on a specific day. The school district could take steps to ensure that student groups maintain appropriate behavior. These regulations must be enforced uniformly on all groups.

AASA, in cooperation with the American Civil Liberties Union, the National Education Association, Americans for Democratic Action, the Joint Baptist Committee, the Christian Legal Society, the American Jewish Congress, and the National Association of Evangelicals, has developed a model policy for school districts that wish to establish a limited open forum. The group has also developed model administrative regulations to help school districts comply with the policy. (See page 55.)

Again, school districts are *not required* to establish a limited open forum. Student activities must simply be related to the curriculum. Although it may be difficult to distinguish between curriculum-related and noncurriculum-related activities, these distinctions can be drawn.

SCHOOL DISTRICT AID TO RELIGIOUS SCHOOLS

In an effort to provide remedial or enrichment instruction to disadvantaged youngsters in religious schools, hundreds of school districts—especially those in urban areas—developed programs in which public school teachers visited school classrooms. In 1985, the Court declared that such religious programs fostered a "symbolic union of government and religion" and declared them unconstitutional.

The Supreme Court considered two separate cases. *Aguilar v. Felton*[133] dealt with a Title I program (now called Chapter 1) administered by the New York City schools. *Grand Rapids v. Ball*[134] concerned a state-funded program in Grand Rapids, Michigan.

In New York City, public school teachers hired under the federal Title I program visited Catholic school classrooms during the regular school day to provide additional instruction in remedial reading and mathematics, as well as other subjects. In the classrooms that were used for Title I instruction, all religious symbols had been temporarily removed.

In Grand Rapids, the public school system used state funds to send public school teachers into nonpublic schools to teach reading, mathematics, and other subjects. The school district leased the classrooms from the schools and required that all religious symbols be removed when the public school teachers were present. In addition, the school district also

---

133. 105 S.Ct. 3232 (1985).
134. 105 S.Ct. 3216 (1985).

MODEL POLICY TO CREATE A LIMITED OPEN FORUM

WHEREAS the United States Congress has enacted the Equal Access Act requiring school boards to permit students to conduct noncurriculum-related meetings during noninstructional time on school premises if the school board permits student groups to so meet; and

WHEREAS the school board hereby expresses its willingness to abide by the Act and enacts this policy to do so. The school board authorizes the superintendent of schools to prepare administrative regulations to create a limited open forum in accordance with related board policy and existing employee contracts.

The board may also wish to set restrictions on time, place, and manner of noncurriculum-related meetings, and to regulate when, where, and how facilities will be available. This permits the board greater control over school facilities.

MODEL ADMINISTRATIVE REGULATIONS

A group of students who wish to conduct a meeting on school premises before or after the instructional day shall file an application for permission for the meeting with the principal of the school building at which the meeting is to be held. The application shall state:

1. The name and address of the student or students and an affirmation by the person preparing the application that the student(s) has voluntarily initiated the meeting.

2. The name of the school sponsor of the meeting, if any.

3. A description of the type of meeting and a statement of purpose and an estimate of expected attendance. This should be accompanied by a copy of any material used to advertise the meeting.

4. If a nonschool attendee is to go to the meeting, his or her name and address must be furnished and the organization with which he or she is affiliated, if any. If the meeting is a religious one, the nonschool attendee shall furnish an affirmation that he or she is not directing, conducting, controlling or regularly attending the activity.

5. The name of the faculty or staff sponsor/monitor of the meeting (if required), and, if the meeting is for religious purposes, affirmation by that person that he or she is not participating in the meeting.

The principal shall approve the meeting if the application is so filled out and if he or she determines that:

1. The meeting is voluntary and student-initiated.

2. There is no sponsorship of the meeting by the school, the government, or its agents or employees.

3. The meeting will not materially and substantially interfere with the orderly conduct of the school's educational activities.

4. Employees of the district are present at religious meetings in a nonparticipatory capacity.

5. Nonschool persons are not directing, controlling or regularly attending the activity.

6. There is no school influence on the form or content of any prayer or religious activity during a meeting for those purposes.

7. No person will be required to participate in prayer or other religious activity during the meeting or activity.

8. No funds will be expended by the school for any such meeting beyond the incidental cost associated with providing meeting space; however, if the school district has an extracurricular pay schedule which provides for compensation for teachers who are required to be present in a supervisory capacity at extracurricular activities, then such teacher will be paid in accordance with such schedule.

9. No employee will be compelled to attend a meeting if the content of the speech at the meeting is contrary to his or her beliefs.

10. If the request is submitted, forms are received at least three days prior to the requested meeting.

---

supported an after-school Community Education Program in nonpublic schools that offered foreign languages, arts instruction, home economics, and other enrichment courses. These Community Education Program courses were taught by regular nonpublic school teachers hired by the school district as part-time teachers.

In *Aguilar v. Felton*, the decision that struck down the New York program, the Court focused on the fact that public school teachers were being sent into nonpublic school classrooms. The need to ensure that such classes had no religious content "inevitably results in the excessive entanglement of church and state." The Court went on to say:

> The principle that the state should not become too closely entangled with the church in the administration of assistance is rooted in two concerns. When the state becomes enmeshed with a given denomination in matters of religious significance, the freedom of religious belief of those who are not adherents of that denomination suffers, even when the governmental purpose underlying the involvement is largely secular. In addi-

tion, the freedom of even the adherents of the denomination is limited by the governmental intrusion into sacred matters.[135]

The New York City program had assigned supervisors to visit each classroom at least once a month. One purpose of these visits was to prevent the Title I program "from being used, intentionally or unwittingly, to inculcate the religious beliefs of the surrounding parochial school."[136] But the Court found that such supervision could require a "permanent and pervasive State presence in the sectarian schools receiving aid."[137] Thus the program was ruled to violate the Establishment Clause because it required excessive entanglement between the state and religion.

The Court used the same reasoning to declare the Grand Rapids programs unconstitutional in *Grand Rapids v. Ball*. The 5-4 decision noted that the students spent their school day moving between religious school and public school classes. "Both take place in the same religious school building and both are largely composed of students who are adherents of the same denomination. In this environment, the students would be unlikely to discern the crucial difference between the classes."[138] Writing for the Court, Justice Brennan explained why such a program violated the Establishment Clause:

> [J]ust as religion throughout history has provided spiritual comfort, guidance and inspiration to many, it can also serve powerfully to divide societies. And to exclude those whose beliefs are not in accordance with particular religions or sects that have from time to time achieved dominance, the solution to this problem adopted by the Framers [of the Constitution] and consistently recognized by this Court is jealously to guard the right of every individual to worship according to the dictates of conscience while requiring the government to maintain a course of neutrality among religions, and between religion and nonreligion. . . .[139]
>
> Government promotes religion as effectively when it fosters a close identification of its power and responsibilities with those of any—or all—religious denominations as when it attempts to inculcate specific religious doctrine. If this identification conveys a message of government endorsement or disapproval of religion, a core purpose of the Establishment Clause is violated. . . .

---

135. 105 S.Ct. 3232, 3237 (1985).
136. *Ibid.*, at 3236, 3237.
137. *Ibid.*, at 3238.
138. 105 S.Ct. 3216, 3227 (1985).
139. *Ibid.*, at 3222.

It follows that an important concern of the [*Lemon*] effects test is whether the symbolic union of church and state is sufficiently likely to be perceived by adherents as an endorsement, and by the nonadherents as a disapproval, of their individual religious choices. The inquiry must be conducted with particular care when many of the citizens perceiving the governmental message are children in their formative years.[140]

Finally, the Court ruled that "the programs in effect subsidize the religious functions of the parochial schools by taking over a substantial portion of their responsibility for teaching secular subjects."[141] The Court did not address the issue of whether the programs would be constitutionally acceptable if the instruction were provided on public school premises. But Justice O'Connor, who dissented from the Court's ruling in the *Aguilar* case, suggested that one possibility for a constitutionally permissible way to provide aid would be "possibly in portable classrooms just over the edge of school property."[142]

If your school district is considering any policy of aid to religious schools in your district, here are some issues to consider:

- Review carefully the three-part test of whether a practice violates the Establishment Clause. The two most recent Supreme Court cases found school practices had a secular *purpose*. Yet one was rejected because its primary *effect* was to advance religion, and the other was rejected largely because it promoted excessive *entanglement* with religion.
- It will be extremely difficult for school districts to justify providing teachers for classes held in religious schools. As the Court said, if this were possible, "the public schools could gradually take on themselves the entire responsibility for teaching secular subjects on religious school premises."

SCHOOL-CHURCH PARTNERSHIPS

Many school districts have developed partnership programs, which use business and community resources to support school programs. In some districts, religious institutions are also included in partnership programs.

These partnerships are based on the philosophy that education is a *shared* responsibility, and that the school, the community, and religion all have a role to play in providing quality education for young people. John Swomley, professor of social ethics at St. Paul School of Theology

---

140. *Ibid.*, at 3226.
141. *Ibid.*, at 3230.
142. 105 S.Ct. 3232, 3248 (1985).

and chairman of the national American Civil Liberties Union Church-State Committee, says, "The churches have an enormous stake in a literate society, in liberal arts education, in a democratically and locally controlled system of free public schools."[143]

Across the country, such partnership programs have addressed a number of different educational concerns. The Interchurch Council of Greater Cleveland has taken an active role in helping schools promote literacy. The Council sponsors a parent reading training program, a parent/child preschool book program, and a high school tutoring program. The Council's Books for People project has distributed more than 237,000 new books to children, as well as needy, ill, or disabled residents of Cleveland. More than 450 churches and synagogues participate in this service project.

Some partnerships focus on communications. Religious institutions have provided a forum for discussion of important educational issues. The Kansas City School District, in cooperation with the Southern Christian Leadership Conference, has developed a public relations campaign on behalf of the public schools. Once a month, the program develops and distributes a half-page flier (suitable for including in a church bulletin) containing information about school programs and resources.

Religious institutions have also made their space available for special programs, such as a suspension center and a teacher center. Some also sponsor programs that use school facilities such as auditoriums and gymnasiums to provide after-school care for children of working parents. A church/school partnership program in Chicago helps adolescent girls establish self-esteem and reduce the high school dropout rate due to pregnancy.

Religious groups have also worked to help recruit volunteers for the public schools and to encourage qualified members to serve on school boards and other school governance committees.

If your school district is considering establishing a program of partnership between school and religious institutions, you may wish to consider these guidelines, developed at the Wingspread Conference on School/Church Partnerships (1985):

• Churches might encourage partnerships with the public schools provided they do not violate court rulings on the separation of church and state.

---

143. John Swomley, "The American Education Debate," *The Christian Century*, Aug. 31, 1983.

- These partnerships might be developed on an inclusive, interfaith basis or through a coalition to ensure that some religious groups do not dominate.
- Church/school partnerships should be based on a foundation of support for helping the community value children in society, since children are often overlooked, neglected or abused, and treated primarily as consumers.
- Any partnership should be developed through open dialogue between the religious community and the public schools on how best to make a positive impact on the community. Common purposes and goals should be sought.
- Public schools should develop good guidelines for church/school partnerships that would prohibit proselytizing and any kind of religious indoctrination.
- Any help provided by outside resource persons should enhance the current curriculum of the schools and be under the direction of the teacher or other appropriate school personnel.
- Churches might provide volunteers to assist schools in dealing with significant issues, such as fund raising; building support for budgets and bond issues; and promoting a commitment to life-long learning, the value of teaching as a vocation, and the importance of a sound system of public education.
- Churches might wish to provide assistance for parents in understanding educational issues and how the public educational system serves as a foundation for a free and democratic society.
- Institutions that prepare the clergy and public school leaders should ensure that graduates understand the importance of the separation of church and state and are prepared to maintain it.
- Language should be developed making it clear that the integrity and independence of the public schools must be maintained, and that church groups should not attempt to dominate the public schools for religious purposes.
- A discussion of ways that schools and churches currently work in partnership might serve as a basis for further discussions.
- School leaders may wish to meet periodically with religious leaders in the community to provide information, answer questions, obtain advice, and seek cooperation on appropriate issues or concerns.

ACKNOWLEDGMENTS

The American Association of School Administrators (AASA) extends its appreciation to the author, Kristen J. Amundson, whose writing skill has brought clarity to complex issues. AASA is also grateful to all who shared information and reviewed the initial manuscript. Among the many who made substantial contributions to this publication are: Marilyn Bendiksen, Supervisor of Extended Programs for the School District of LaCrosse, Wisconsin; Wes Bodin of the St. Louis Park Public Schools in Minnesota; Craig Conrath, lawyer; Boardman Kathan of Prospect, Connecticut; Charles Kniker of Iowa State University, who is editor of *Religion & Public Education*, published by the National Council on Religion and Public Education; Patricia Lines, Education Commission of the States; Nicholas Piediscalzi of Wright State University; Nanette Roberts, General Secretary of the United Church Board of Homeland Ministries; John Swomley, School of Theology, Kansas City, Missouri and chairperson, Church-State Committee, American Civil Liberties Union; Roger Wangen, Minnesota State Department of Education; and Thayer Warshaw of Andover, Massachusetts.

Religion in the Public Schools is dedicated to former AASA Senior Associate Executive Director, James R. Kirkpatrick, who was an advocate for this publication and contributed numerous ideas and insights prior to his untimely death.

Cindy Tursman, editor of *The School Administrator*, handled editing and production for this book. AASA Associate Executive Director, Gary Marx, served as Project Director.